THE SECRETS OF DATING YOUR BUSINESS

The Secrets of
DATING YOUR
BUSINESS

HOW BUILDING RELATIONSHIPS IS THE KEY
TO HAPPINESS AND WILD SUCCESS

Miriam Steketee

LIONCREST
PUBLISHING

THE SECRETS OF DATING YOUR BUSINESS

How Building Relationships Is the Key to Happiness and Wild Success

ISBN   978-1-5445-1729-2 *Paperback*

          978-1-5445-1728-5 *Ebook*

CONTENTS

I've learned that people will forget what you said, people will forget what you did, but people will never forget how you made them feel.

—MAYA ANGELOU

INTRODUCTION

Nine years ago, I was a new mom, and lonely in a job that undervalued and underappreciated me. Nine years ago, I was dealing with so much credit card debt and law school loans (courtesy of my darling husband) that I didn't know how we would get out from under it. And nine years ago, I took a leap of faith, said yes to a new opportunity, and ended up more fulfilled, successful, and happy than I ever thought possible.

Don't roll your eyes just yet because, girl, it wasn't easy.

I wish I could say that the moment I took that leap that the skies opened up and my life changed instantly, but I'd be lying. My rise from hot mess to network marketing success wasn't simple or glamorous. It took hard work, setbacks and fresh starts, wins, losses, doubts, successes, many, *many* conversations over martinis, and a hell of a lot of dates: good and bad.

Let me rewind: in a previous life I was a professional dancer with Broadway dreams. I jetted from audition to audition, but my lack of a steady job wasn't helping my student loans or astronomical credit card bills, so in between dancing gigs, I worked part time in real estate, worked events on weekends, and waitressed to bring in extra money. It was just as fabulous as you can imagine. After a few years of the hustle, I was still struggling to make ends meet, and I gave up on my childhood dream. My confidence was down, and my money woes were up, so I decided to do the "sensible thing" and get a job that paid a salary and offered a 401(k).

It broke my heart to give up on my dream. But I always throw myself into everything I do, and so by thirty, my career in real estate was taking off and I was already a managing director for a top firm in New York City—I even had an office on Park Avenue. I looked like I had it all, but in reality, I was struggling big time! After my son Sebastian was born, my discontent only intensified. I wanted to be with him all the time, but quitting wasn't an option (we still had debt, and the economy was crashing), so I found myself stuck in the land of career-mom confusion: I needed to find a way out of the corporate world, but I also needed to make money.

That's when a friend shared an opportunity to join her in

her new network marketing company. My first thought was, "Hell no." It wasn't the right time. I was a busy new mom working full time in Manhattan. I had every reason to say no, but I couldn't stop thinking, "What if?"

What if?

So I went for it.

It took four years for me to go from not knowing a thing to becoming a top earner in my company. It's a messy and beautiful story that has taught me so much about myself and how to fall in love over and over again with my business. And that is the secret to my success: to serve others and treat everyone I encounter with love, respect, and a giving heart. Fall in love with people and the process rather than money and power. When you lead with love, your life begins to change, and doors open up for you that you never knew existed.

Think about it: workplaces sell products or services, but it's the people who are the heart and the soul of a company. It's the people you need to grow, motivate, and inspire. When you work with people you love and want to support, it's the ultimate joy. You need to be patient with your relationships, court them, treat them with respect, decide which ones are worthy and which ones are better to walk away from and try again. In the dating game, you can't go out on three bad dates, call it quits, and become a nun. The same thing goes for business: you can't expect instant miracles, immediate milestones, or to become a millionaire overnight. You can't even expect that in your first few years.

When people first start building a business, they seem to focus on gaining new customers and making contacts instead of focusing on the long term. They don't build and grow relationships for the future. I've discovered that the best way to create a successful business is to "date" it: pursue it, love on it, give it attention, and commit to it as you would the person you want to date and marry. It won't always be romantic. You will be nervous at times, and even think about breaking up with it, but in the end, it will be worth it, and you two can grow old together. I want to help you do just that.

You see, I made a lot of mistakes when I began my network marketing business. I had a slow start and didn't have much financial success for many months, even though I was working hard. As it turns out, my initial lack of success was because I was working in all the wrong places.

I made a list of people who I thought would be great in this business, but I didn't share the opportunity with them because I wanted to be successful first. I focused on mass marketing, cold calling, and posting ads. I was so scared of what the people I knew might think of me, or what they would think if my pitch wasn't perfect, so I avoided them like the plague. I didn't take advantage of my warm network. Honestly, I had a hot network, too, but I only sought out prospects from my cold one—I was afraid to approach the people I knew and truly wanted to work with because it was easier to be rejected by strangers. It's like dating strangers with great profile pics as opposed to going for that nice guy or the friend who makes you laugh a lot. You don't want to mess up what you already have, so you venture out to see what else is out there. The perfect dream guy is in front of you, and you're too chicken to give him a try!

After playing it safe for a while, I realized other people in my industry were experiencing a lot of success, and I wasn't. I needed to figure out what I was doing wrong, so I reached out and did what I do best: I made a connection and asked a lot of questions. I talked with a few of them and soon realized I needed to get out of my own way and stop prejudging my family and friends. I needed to approach everyone I knew in a strong, confident, and powerful manner and then let them decide what they'd like to do.

That's what I did, and now I am a top earner in my industry. I have fallen more times than I could imagine, and each time, I came back stronger. I train and mentor thousands of consultants across the globe, and I share the same secret recipe I divulge here: success is about people and how you build relationships with them.

WHY I'M WRITING THIS BOOK

I know how it feels to be trapped in a corporate structure or in a career that just doesn't feel right, knowing that there is another path but feeling lost, confused, or scared to make it happen. That's why I love helping others on that journey to get unstuck to find success, monetarily and within. It's what motivates me, what drives me, and why I work so hard to build the network marketing business I have today. I've created a team of more than sixteen thousand entrepreneurs filled with a positive culture and a camaraderie that so many women are lacking in the workplace.

I also love to share. I'm not one of those women who keeps everything close to the vest, and I believe there is enough opportunity in this world for everyone. When I find an awesome new Mexican restaurant, I tell everyone I know! Fabulous deal on a beach coverup? I send my friends the link. I've benefited from the wisdom of people in my life and want to give back. I've coached thousands of entrepreneurs over the years, done hundreds of trainings, and know what works in this business and what doesn't. I want to share my secrets to success with you.

In this book, you'll learn new skills and improve upon the ones you already have. You'll learn what you need to do for yourself and what you need to do for others. You'll learn how to approach different types of people and how to build relationships with each one. In the following pages, I'll share my failures, my successes, and all I've learned through trial and error. At the end, you'll also be fully equipped to embark on your journey with clearly defined dos and don'ts. It doesn't matter if you're starting an online or network marketing business, writing a blog, or opening a retail store. This book will help you create a plan and teach you what you need to know to be successful and happy.

If you're feeling hesitant, know this: I started with nothing, but I was able to build something extraordinary. My business allowed me to make enough money to leave my job in corporate America and to give myself and my husband financial options and time freedom. No matter your background, I believe this is possible for you, too. The beauty of network marketing and this new age of social selling is that a person's educational or professional background doesn't dictate their success—personality, grit, integrity, and a desire to learn will. No matter where you went to college or what degree you have, everyone begins on equal ground in this industry. It doesn't matter what you've done in the past; all that matters is what you do today.

An independent business can provide a steady source of primary or supplemental income while giving you the freedom to decide where and when you will work. I'm here to encourage and empower you to make a change in your life, if that's what you're after. I want to help you nurture and build a business that you fall in love with and help you enjoy the journey as well.

Are you ready to put yourself out there? Let's get started!

PART I

Love Yourself First

Chapter One

ARE YOU READY TO PUT YOURSELF OUT THERE?

What if?

What if you stopped worrying about what everyone else thinks?

What if you stop judging people based on what they look like on paper or in person?

What if something/someone is not too good to be true, and it's just that good?

Playing the what-if game has helped me break through a

barrier of fear and change my life. When I flip the script in my head and say, "What if?" everything shifts and rings the confidence bell. My relationship with myself, my prospects, and anyone who comes within three feet of me starts to soar. It's made me a proud, fearless she-warrior ready to love on anyone I can! That's what my job is and yours, too. Get others to think, "What if? Could this be a game changer for me? Could my life be different or better?"

I have my parents to thank for instilling a growth mindset in me. I was born in Brooklyn, New York, to two Russian immigrants, Boris and Lyudmila (Lucy for short), and moved to the New Jersey suburbs when I was seven. My parents were strict, but they showed me the true meaning of hustle, grit, failure, starting again, and success. They encouraged and mentored me, and instilled a fearlessness in me to ask for what I wanted. My parents had a vast appreciation for the opportunities in this country, which was a recurring theme in the stories they told me about growing up in the Communist Soviet Union, where a factory worker and a doctor earned a similar income and entrepreneurship was considered a crime, punishable by jail time. There was little to dream of or hope for.

When they came to the United States, they couldn't believe the possibilities. They thought, "You can start a business? You can get bonuses? You can ask for more money?" Even though both of my parents had great careers in computer software development in Manhattan, my dad was all about finding opportunities to create wealth and leave a legacy for his children. He had other businesses and viewed side hustles as "adventures," and he always encouraged me to start my own. It was that excitement for opportunity that made a lasting impression on me and was what fueled my own drive.

In the eyes of my parents and friends, I had accomplished quite a bit by age thirty. I married my college sweetheart, Randy, the best damn guy in the world, and I had an executive position at one of the top real estate companies in NYC. From the outside, it looked like I had it all, but in reality, it wasn't the life I had envisioned. Something gnawed at me nightly, and I knew deep down something wasn't right.

I was making good money, giving my all for my company, trying to meet quotas and climbing the corporate ladder, but I was unfulfilled and knew this wasn't "it." I worked my tail off day in and day out, twenty-four seven. I had numbers to hit, and I worked around the clock to meet them. But here's the thing, once you met your quotas, upper management would increase them the next quarter, making it harder to chase your goals! Why was the reward for my good performance a push to work even harder? There was no celebration, little recognition, or even a positive outlook when you hit your goals either. It was such a backward system—instead of motivating me, they added more stress and put me in a position where I didn't want to work too hard.

To make matters worse, my husband had just graduated from law school, and we were repaying the crushing loans, the economy was crashing, our credit card bills were getting larger every month, and we were trying to get pregnant. I needed to find a way out of the corporate world, but I also needed to make real money—and a lot of it. So instead of quitting, I recalled something my dad always said, "Just ask for a promotion! What's the worst that can happen? They say no."

The fact that I was one of the youngest people on the management team didn't stop me. We needed more money. Period. I decided to put my big-girl panties on and just ask. A few weeks later, I got a call—someone had quit, and they needed a replacement fast. After a few interviews, I moved up another step on the ladder and landed a job as the manager of the Park Avenue office.

Hooray! My dad was right! I just had to ask.

THE PROMOTION

I was so excited about my new position and the big raise, better title, bigger and better office, Blackberry, and new challenges. Great responsibilities were on the horizon, and

I was going to bring home a lot more bacon. Then, a few days before I started the new role, my boss introduced me to my new counterpart.

"Miriam, this is Greg. You two will be co-managing this office. Well, he'll be the managing director, and you will be the manager—you'll report to him."

I was stunned. I felt sick. I couldn't believe they just found an agent with no managerial experience—and he was going to be my boss! *What?* I was confused as to why senior leadership didn't think I could handle this level of responsibility on my own. I had already basically done the job for the last two years at another office. Later, someone told me that a little birdy said they wanted "some testosterone" to head the office, and I lacked what was required to be a managing director at that time: a penis.

Instead of starting an awesome new role and independently managing an office, I spent months training Greg. Through the course of our many conversations, we became good friends, and at one point, we talked about salaries. I found out that he made 50 percent more than I did! *What the #$%^?*

On top of that, I felt lonely. When I worked as a part-time agent, I had friends at the office. We would go to open houses, lunches, or happy hours together. After the promotion, I did my best to maintain my previous friendships in the other office and connect with new people, but the dynamics had changed. I had also gotten pregnant and was one of the first of all my friends to have a baby, so I felt like the odd woman out trying to figure out the whole pregnant-to-working-mom thing.

The pay disparity and this loneliness solidified the thought I'd been having for quite a while: I needed to make a change.

MY TURNING POINT

I've always been an entrepreneur at heart (I ruled the babysitting scene in middle school) and was determined to find another way to make money—a better way. I had no idea where to look, but I knew I had to start. I began searching for other jobs and side gigs. I confessed to an old friend in a Facebook chat that I was miserable at my job and was asking how she was doing as a new working mom.

She told me she was also over corporate America, and alongside her advertising career, she had started a side hustle with a network marketing company and asked if I was interested—no prior experience was needed. My initial reaction was, "Hell no, I don't want to throw cheesy parties and sell to my friends." I told her I would think about it, and to be honest, I did. It wasn't just a throwaway line you use to turn down someone in the nicest way possible. The more research I did on the industry, the more compelling it became. The possibilities she described were enticing, and honestly, what other options did I have in the little time I had free? I spoke to my father and my husband, who both gave me the green light and nudged me to give it a try. So in a moment of courage, I said yes. I was more than ready to jump off the corporate hamster wheel.

I became more hopeful when I found out that the company was founded and run by two women who believed in female empowerment. After working at a company primarily run by men, I was ready for a refreshing change. I began to learn the business during little pockets of free time during the day. In the evenings, I took advantage of the fact that I was nursing an eight-month-old and had no social life.

Real talk: it wasn't easy. I felt vulnerable starting something new, but after several months, I started to find some success. I didn't have a fast start, and I made many mistakes, but I learned from them. I used them to guide me, and I never gave up. Because I embraced a growth mindset, my business grew exponentially over time. And after several years, I was financially free and making more money than I could have ever imagined.

Over the last nine years, I've developed an extremely successful home-based direct sales business and a team of thousands of incredible women and men who are now dear friends. I didn't build this network by hoping and wishing to make contacts, or by relying on family and friends for their support; instead, I looked for opportunities to meet new people, cultivated new relationships, and nurtured the ones I already had. I became a person of the people. Getting to know and falling in love with the process, the people, and the business. I believe that this—along with building a positive business and team culture—is what has made me successful.

I used to think it was impossible to have a lucrative career and have the freedom to spend time with my family and friends. And I would have been right had I not been willing to change. My path forward was clear: keep building my business and let *nothing* stand in my way.

IS YOUR CUP BEING FILLED?

We work to make money, but it's also because we want and need a sense of fulfillment. This is the driving force behind all that we do, and we need to feel valued and self-affirmed in more than one area of life. For instance, stay-at-home moms might be fulfilled as mothers, but there might be another part of their life that is lacking. Corporate career moms may love the sense of accomplishment but might wish they had more time for their personal lives. Fulfillment comes from helping others in meaningful ways and seeing the impact you have made.

That pit in my stomach at the real estate firm kept growing in step with my lack of fulfillment, and I don't think I'm unique in feeling that way. I believe there is an absence of joy in much of corporate America because employees rarely get to see the end result of what they are working on. Their contribution gets lost in many layers, and they don't receive any fulfillment from the end product, nor do they get recognition for the small or large contribution they made. In corporate America and in most professions, you are paid a salary, and it doesn't matter how many people you help. You could excel or not do a good job at all, and you still get paid the same amount. Sound familiar?

I wanted to see the impact of my contribution and feel that sense of happiness and fulfillment from helping others. I wanted to give back in the world, be appreciated, and make money on my own terms.

This is why so many corporate professionals and even teachers, lawyers, and doctors seek career pivots and excel at network marketing. The business model is totally different: I share my products with people, and when they use them and enjoy the results, I find fulfillment. When I share the business side with others, they might decide to join, and I help them get started and mentor them through a partnership. They earn commission on their personal sales and team sales and I earn a commission too, when they are successful. The more people I help, the more people succeed. When people succeed, they feel fulfilled and work harder, and so do I! You don't have any bosses or people to report to—it's a wonderful community of entrepreneurs helping one another.

IT'S NOT ABOUT ME; IT'S ABOUT US

This was the biggest mindset breakthrough for me. I remember a time when I was gunning for a promotion. And it wasn't just any promotion; this promotion came with a rewards trip to San Francisco and Sonoma Wine country! Up until the moment my promotion was announced, I had pictured a huge celebration: I'd be surrounded by a crowd of people, we'd have champagne, and my phone would be blowing up. Instead, I hit that new rank right in the middle of Hurricane Sandy, when many people were living with no power, heat, or internet. Needless to say, my focus quickly shifted.

A few months later, I realized that even though the moment of winning was a letdown, the two years I spent working toward my huge goal were filled with joy, personal growth, and wonderful moments. Everything I had done—the phone calls, the training, the friendship and relationship building, and even the rejection—had all made the journey exciting. The business itself made me happy. I didn't just find joy in hitting the milestone and earning the trip—I found it in everything in between.

We've all heard stories about people winning the lottery and then going bankrupt. We've all been shocked when a famous, rich, or successful person fails hard or goes off the edge. We thought they had it all—looks, money, and the hot guy—but there was still something wrong. I believe success in life is about finding happiness in the journey and not just in fleeting moments. I do my best to enjoy the experience of building my business, and I've let go of the notion that I'll only be happy once I'm successful. I want to be happy and fulfilled right now! I want to feel worthy right now! And I want to help you find happiness in your journey. I want you to move forward with a positive outlook!

I meet women all the time who complain about their current situation. Some don't have any money saved, others haven't received a raise in years. Some left careers to stay home with their kids, and now they only receive an "allowance." Others work to afford childcare and to make ends meet. Many of these women are looking for more. They know they deserve more. More greatness, happiness, fulfillment. We deserve to make money, and lots of it, but money itself won't bring happiness. What it does bring are options and choices, and that's what everyone is seeking. That's what we want and need! Feeling fulfilled in a career and having enough money to not be in a constant state of panic is the new definition of success. Is that your definition, too? Think about it. If that's what you want, there's no reason to not go after it!

Take a moment to ask yourself these questions:

- What do you want more of?
- What do you want less of?
- What does your dream future look like?
- What does your ideal day-to-day look like?
- What would make you love your life?
- Are you in a good place in your career?
- Are you happy in your job?
- What relationships make you happy?
- Which relationships stress you out?
- When you have X more money saved, what would change?

Chapter Two

WHAT'S YOUR HAPPILY EVER AFTER?

Money doesn't buy happiness. We hear this phrase a lot. But let's be honest, people—money does provide security and stability, which means less stress. Getting out of debt and having enough socked away in the bank for a rainy day is really nice. I know, because there was a point in my life when I got into financial hot water.

When I first married Randy, I thought we were living on top of the world. We were madly in love and lived in the moment; we didn't think too much about the future and enjoyed what we had. He was thirty years old and studying to be a lawyer, which made me the breadwinner at twenty-seven, (although I use that phrase loosely, because we didn't have much money and lived primarily on credit cards). It didn't matter to me at the time, though, because I was in love, and I was about to be the wife of a *lawyer*. I mean, hello, it doesn't get better than that! Ha! (So I thought.)

Randy was next in line for a high-profile attorney position at a prestigious New York City law firm, but that dream quickly crashed with the economy in 2008. Instead of hiring, the law firm was firing half of their attorneys. It was a scary, uncertain time, amplified by the fact that his impending law school debt was about to hit us hard. Thankfully, Randy found a job through a good friend at the New York Stock Exchange, but the pay was as unsexy as the job. He basically made just enough to cover his student loans and the rent. We never had money left over and were entering what would be many years of rising debt. Good times!

OPPOSITES ATTRACT

Growing up, Randy's experiences with money were quite different from mine: his family always lived within their means, paid cash or check for mostly everything, and carried essentially no debt. On the flip side, my parents had a double mortgage on their home to pay for my sister's and my college tuition and were big on using credit cards... and getting points. They weren't careless. They worked extremely hard and were optimistic—no, confident—that all would be okay in the end. Randy was so not like that.

Even though we'd been a couple for seven years, I'd always had my money, and he'd had his. It was easier that way. But then we went through the application process to rent our first apartment together, and Randy found out my credit score. *Eek!* This was a major skeleton in the closet: a bunch of credit cards, with very large balances, and no way to pay them off. It wasn't pretty.

It was a sad day when the credit reports arrived and I was officially busted. He was in shock and, welp, I was a fraud! There he was, all innocent, scraping by and trying to live frugally with what he made, and I was spending money without a care in the world. That night, as tears streamed down my face, he made me cut up my credit cards one by one. And poof, there they went into the trash. Gone.

Oh. My. God. This was for real! I remember despairing and wondered what the hell I was going to do.

I spent years as a dancer, working events, and in real estate had created a "credit mindset," because many times, I wasn't paid right away. In real estate in particular, when a deal was in the works, sometimes I didn't get paid for a few months!

As badly as I wanted to keep my cards, I realized we would never get ahead if I continued to be careless with finances. I needed to find ways to save money, but I also needed to find ways to make more of it. I knew I needed to be more in control of my financial destiny and get back to my entrepreneurial roots.

I'M A SIDE HUSTLER, BABY

Finances can often make or break a relationship, and I don't want you to make the same mistakes I did. Don't wait until you get married to start planning for the future. If you're already married and haven't planned, talk to a financial advisor or, even better, a fiduciary.

Think about where you are today and why starting a side hustle could be smart for you. Ask yourself the following questions:

- Are you in debt? If so, how much debt do you have?
- Do you have any money in savings or investments?
- How much are you putting into your savings each month?
- Are you financially comfortable or making just enough to get by?
- Do you have growth opportunities in your career to make more money in the future?
- If you were to lose your job, do you have enough money set aside for a period of unemployment?

Since my parents were always open with our financial

situation, I discovered at an early age that life with two salaries was good, but it wasn't usually enough to provide for your dream life. This is why my father always had his side businesses. When our family did well, we were stress free, went on amazing trips, and bought new clothes. But when we didn't do well, and my dad lost money on a deal, or my parents wouldn't get their bonus, there was tension and fighting in the house. Our family conversations often went like this: "Since there were no bonuses this year, you can't get new clothes for spring. There's no extra money, and you'll have to take your lunch to school, or there will be no camp or family vacation this summer." It was quite a lifestyle change, and I never liked it, but it taught me a lot at a young age.

It's unfortunate, but you can't rely on an annual raise anymore. And if you haven't been saving 5 to 10 percent of what you make, it's time to start. If you're unable to do so in your current situation, or your 10 percent looks like one hundred bucks a month, then it's probably time for a side hustle. Starting a business adds an extra stream of income to your life and will set you up for the future. Being an entrepreneur is pretty much a necessity in our current market.

If you want and need to build something for yourself, you can. Just make up your mind and decide to do it. Open your eyes and see all the opportunities around you! Stop telling yourself that you're stuck in a situation until you retire, or until X, Y, or Z happens, because guess what? People retire, and they can still be unhappy or in a bad financial place. Pensions and promises of a secure future income are disappearing. That means you should start building a nest egg today instead of waiting until later or someday. When you keep saying "someday," that someday will never happen.

Starting a business might sound scary to you, but trust me, making extra money is fun and empowering. Being your own boss is a gift. Maybe you'll learn something about yourself. Maybe you'll meet some truly great people. Maybe you'll grow as a person. Maybe you will change your financial situation and become more fulfilled. Maybe you will fuel a passion you never knew you had. If you aren't where you want to be in life, or you feel like you're stuck, stressed, or you just want more, and you don't know what the more is, a business could be just the thing you need!

BE RESOURCEFUL

Confidence can open doors for you, but the reality is that you do need some money to build a business. You might not need a ton—typically, online businesses have a low overhead, but there will be expenses, and you won't have a lot of income at first. A business, after all, is an investment in your future, and you need to be as resourceful as possible. Some people give up too quickly because they think they need to invest a lot of money into a new venture, and that's simply not true.

First, look at the concept of resources in a new light. Our default thinking is that we have to pay money in exchange for services, and that isn't always the case. Many of us have friends or family members who will gladly exchange one service for another, or for a favor. If you take the time to look around, you'll likely discover you are surrounded by an amazing number of people who want to help you. I understand you might be hesitant or nervous to ask people for favors, but it might be the only option you have. And how will you know if you don't ask?

When I first got started, I needed to advertise and get the buzz going about my business in New York City. One problem: I had no budget for it. We were strapped for cash, and remember, I had no more credit cards! I reached out to a friend who was a talented graphic designer, and I asked her if we could make a deal: if she'd make flyers for me, I'd give her a free product in return.

I also had to be resourceful when it came to renting space for one of my first events. It's no secret that renting in New York City is expensive, so I posted a request on Facebook asking if anyone had an event space I could use for free. It was a bold request, but tons of people responded. They viewed my request as an opportunity to promote their business through my event. I worked out an amazing deal with a friend who was a restaurant event coordinator, and I began hosting events there on a regular basis.

Another example of where you can swap time and resources is with childcare. Many moms who are starting a business do it after hours from their full-time job, or around their kids' naps and schedules, but let's face the truth. It's hard to build a business and make appointments with a screaming kid in the background. You'll need childcare at least once a week, so why not swap with another mom? Watch their kid for three hours, and then they can watch yours. Or ask a local teen to become a mother's helper, and they can play with your child while you work, and you can pay them half of what you would pay a typical sitter. Don't be afraid to ask for help from family and friends—they can be your most precious resource!

Chapter Three

WHAT'S HOLDING YOU BACK?

As I moved through my early years, my parents, Russian immigrants, drilled their mantra for success in my brain: good grades, good college, good job. Work hard, play hard. And so, like a good daughter, I followed suit. I studied hard, I trained hard in dance class, and I went to a top college. After graduation, I moved to New York City to pursue my love of dance and try to make a career of it. I had eyes on Broadway; it was my dream.

To support myself between dance classes, auditions, and gigs, I worked parttime in real estate, danced for an event company on the weekends, baby sat, and worked as a waitress and bartender. And after three years, I was still struggling to make a real income and make it big.

I decided that the Broadway dream was too difficult to achieve.

The negative voices of family and friends, as well as my own poor self-talk, led me to give up. "Just quit already, Miriam!" "You will never make it!" Those little voices from outside and within were too much for my twenty-five-year-old ego to take in. The crazy part is that I was always that girl who pushed my friends and family to never give up, to reach for the stars, to dream big and make lemonade from lemons. But deep inside, I didn't have the belief in myself. It still kills me when I think about "What if?" but then maybe I wouldn't be where I am today. Perspective! Now I know that it could take ten to twenty years to find success as a professional dancer, but I got impatient and discouraged after only three short years. I gave it up. It still pains me today, and I don't want you to live a life of regret!

After coaching thousands of women and building my business, these are the most common pitfalls that hold women back in business (and in love):

TRAP #1: LISTENING TO NEGATIVE THOUGHTS

Negative self-talk will ruin your dreams. I know, because it almost ruined mine.

When I decided to build my business, I saw this as my

second chance to make my dreams come true, but I had to build myself up before I could move forward. I made a firm decision to let go of the past and stop the negative self-talk.

This is one of the most important things you need to do before you can start building your business. All those voices that live in your head because of things that happened in your past? Get rid of them. I understand that you may have had bad experiences as a child, or when you were in high school, or from an ex, or a parent, or a friend. I get it. It sucks, and it might still sting, but you can't keep carrying it with you. If an ex-boyfriend influenced a negative mindset, you have to break free of that. Carrying the past makes you scared of change, and you might even be more afraid of success than you are of failure.

Here are common negative thoughts:

- "I could never do that."
- "I'm not as good as she is."
- "I don't have enough time."

Here's how to flip it in your mind:

- "It wouldn't hurt to try something new. Worst case, I learn, and best case, I find something new, make some money, and learn more about myself!"
- "Wow, she is so successful! That's an inspiration and

reminder to me that hard work does pay off. If I work hard, maybe I, too, can be successful."

- "I am so busy, but I hate being so busy. Maybe starting something new will allow me to make extra income and alleviate stress and give me options for more time."

TRAP #2: BECOMING THE QUEEN OF EXCUSES

When I first begin to encourage women and tell them it's possible to build something for themselves, they often ask why they should start a business. After hundreds of conversations, I've come to realize that the question isn't, "Why?" It's, "Why not?" Why not you? Why can't you have it all? Why can't you have the guy (or girl), the friends, the business, and the family? You can.

First, stop making excuses. I'll say it again: stop making excuses. We have excuses for anything and everything, but we need to realize that superstars like Madonna and Beyoncé have the same number of hours in the day as we do, and they get it done. They had the same hours before they were stars. We may not have the same resources that they have to get things done, but a wise person once told me, "It's not about your resources; it's about your resourcefulness." You can overcome it!

Change is hard, but you need to do it for your future because you're worth it. Let me put it to you this way: you probably had a girlfriend—or maybe it was you—who had "that boyfriend" who was terrible for her. He was rude and treated her badly. You know exactly what I'm talking about. You and your friends all knew it, and your girlfriend knew it, but she kept going back to him, over and over again. It was frustrating, right? You just wanted to shake her and say, "Get over him! You deserve better! Let's get you looking cute and go out tonight. There's someone else out there for you!" Despite your disapproval, your friend was afraid to make a change, and she kept going back to what she didn't truly want. It was easier for her to make excuses and stick with what wasn't working. Don't let this be you.

When I first started my business, I was in survival mode—maybe even panic mode. I had an eight-month-old baby who wasn't sleeping, I was working a full-time job, I was paying someone else to take care of my baby and send me pictures of his milestones (which only compounded my baby blues), and I felt like I was burning the candle at both ends. I didn't have money to throw around, I didn't have anything in savings, and I definitely didn't want to keep taking my own lunch to work. I had every excuse in the world for this not to work.

Here are some of my favorites:

- "I'm too old to try something new."
- "I don't have time."

- "I'm not a salesperson."
- "I don't know enough people."

Sound familiar?

Radically successful people face the same failure traps. Oprah was told she was "too emotional" for TV. Walt Disney was fired for "not being creative enough." And Steve Jobs dropped out of college after one semester. These examples should clearly tell you that you're not too old, too shy, too this, or too that to start something new. It's not too late! If you're not happy or you're not financially stable, something needs to change. Stop telling yourself that you can't do it. That's BS.

It wasn't easy to get where I am today, but every moment was worth it. This business has provided experiences for me and my family that I wouldn't trade for anything. We've traveled the world and made memories that may not have been possible with other jobs. I am so glad I didn't listen to the negative voices and followed my heart, and that is all I want for you!

TRAP #3: PLAYING THE WAITING GAME

Throughout my coaching and mentoring, I've discovered one thing many of us women have in common: we always seem to be waiting for something. We think happiness will come once we meet a certain milestone or accomplishment. Or that it will be handed to us. (It's often called the "tiara syndrome.") You know how it is. You think, "I'll be happy once I leave this job and buy that house," or, "I'll be happy when I get a promotion at work." We think achievements will make us happy, but they are just a fleeting moment in time. We have to realize that happiness is found in the journey. We need to find happiness in all that we do while we work toward a goal or destination.

Before you start and commit to your business, you need to get rid of the words, "I'm gonna." That phrase pops up all the time when I'm coaching. People say they're "gonna" do something as soon as X, Y, or Z happens. You will never build a business with that mindset. This is similar to waiting for happiness, but in this case, they won't take action until a certain thing happens first.

I've found that building a business is not just about making money. It's also about pushing yourself to your limits and discovering your full potential. It's fulfilling to create something that is entirely yours and have it be successful. We sometimes hear about people who get interviewed on their deathbeds and say, "I wish I would have taken that risk." I don't want to be that person; I don't want to have regrets at the end of the day, and I don't want you to have them either. No more, "I'm gonna do this," or "I'm gonna do that." No more, "I'm waiting for this," or, "I'm waiting for that." Let's focus on today. Let's focus on you. And let's start to grow!

TRAP #4: THINKING YOU DON'T HAVE WHAT IT TAKES

You've likely heard the phrase, "Fake it till you make it." I'm a huge proponent of this approach. Having a growth mindset will push you to say yes, try new things, fail, succeed, and most importantly, grow! When you are a single gal and you put yourself out there, you need to have your head held high and your confidence level at a ten, with the mindset of, "I am the best thing you will ever meet, so you better treat me well, or bye-bye!"

The same thing goes when you're building your business. You have to exude the vibe that you've already accomplished a lot and you are successful, and you have to display this with your whole heart and soul. You can't give the impression that you're simply "trying to get there" even if you still are. I'm not suggesting that you lie about your level of success, but sharing your products, service, or opportunities with enthusiasm and confidence can make your dreams become reality. Because at the end of the day, what is success? Success is merely an accomplishment, and you set that accomplishment, right? You got one customer. *Success!* See, that was easy, wasn't it?

I learned the hard way that talent alone won't make your

dreams come true. Having a growth mindset and the willingness to say yes, however, will. When I first started my business, I felt like I was reliving my dancing days. I felt so uneasy for months and dealt with rejection. I threw spaghetti at the wall, hoping something would stick. However, I knew that if I kept going and kept practicing, eventually I'd be successful. I had to be. And I was, but it took a long time. If you can do the same and embrace challenges and new opportunities with confidence, I promise that you will learn and master them as you go. This attitude has helped me become a yes-girl!

Many people I coach in business will tell me, "I'm not good at this," or "I've never done that before." I encourage them to change their mindset and reframe their words. Instead, I tell them to say, "I'm not good at that yet, but I will be. I'll do my best to get there, and I'll work on it until I've got it. Failure is not an option." It's important to realize that nobody excels on day one—we're going to have failures along the way. Singers, athletes, and anyone who is accomplished or skilled probably struggled at first, but it was necessary to pave the road to success. Accept that you might not be good at something in the beginning, but you will be.

TRAP #5: BEING AFRAID OF COMMITMENT

Nobody likes to fail, but we know it's a real possibility when we start something new. In order to protect ourselves from embarrassment, we tell people we're "giving something a try," or we're waiting to "see how it goes." This is a huge no-no. In dating, if you tell your friends you might be open to dating, is anyone going to rush to set you up? No way. It's rare for us to say with complete certainty, "I'm going to do this, and I'm going to be that." When starting your own business, it's absolutely necessary to step forward with an attitude of certainty and commitment. After all, if you don't believe you are committed, how are others going to believe it? You have to act like a leader from the very beginning, even if you don't have anyone to lead. Believe in what you're doing, and share the excitement so your energy becomes contagious!

A key element of success in any profession is trust, and choosing confidence is a good way to build it. If you waver in your words or attitude, people will have a hard time trusting you, and trust and belief is everything! Think about it: teachers have to sell what they have to offer to students and parents, and lawyers have to do the same with their clients. I've found that the people who can develop trust with others are the ones who get ahead.

Going back to my performing days, if you really wanted to make it, you had to become a "triple threat," which meant you had to dance, act, and sing. And you had to do all three of those things well. Unfortunately, I sabotaged myself because I had a fear of public speaking, and that fear led me to typecast myself as a dancer only. I was so comfortable expressing myself through movement that I never took the initiative to get over my stage fright with speaking in public. Ninety-nine percent of people are scared of that, too, yet with practice, you can get over it. I certainly have, and so can you!

Looking back, I think it's crazy that I quit so early, because now I give speeches to large groups all the time, and I have trained thousands of people. Of course, I still get butterflies in my stomach, but I love it. It makes me feel alive—it's like I'm performing again but in a different way. Butterflies = growth, and growth is good. You can only get better if you fail over and over and over again, but you continue to improve each time.

I definitely regret giving up my Broadway dream, but I was too young to realize that I could grow and become better. I didn't need to be born with a natural gift. I could have trained hard and expanded my possibilities, but I didn't have that growth mindset. Like a broken record, I kept saying, "If I don't get this role, I'm quitting." I said that to myself before every audition, when I should have been saying, "I'm going to be amazing. They're going to love me!" We need to apply this mindset in everything we do—it doesn't matter if we're going in for an audition, starting a new job, or going into a new business venture. You've got to have a winning mentality. Just say yes!

Chapter Four

BE THE BEST VERSION OF YOURSELF

You are your brand. You are the impression you leave on people. So that means you need to work on yourself. If you were the mean girl back in high school, it's time to show people that you've changed. It's time to rebuild trust. You might need to repair some relationships. Pick up the phone and check on people. When you see a need, meet it.

If you're unhappy, or if there are people in your life who aren't the best versions of themselves, surround yourself with others who embrace a growth mindset. Hang out with people you want to emulate. Think about the people you know who don't wait to be asked for help; they just help. That's who you want to be! Being kind and doing something positive is better than doing nothing. Don't get stuck on what to do. Just do.

You were put on this earth for a reason. Remember that! You have a gift to give, and you can only give it if you fall in love with yourself first! As the saying goes, you can only find love when you love yourself, and you can only build a successful business when you project the confidence and compassion needed to build relationships. Here are some ways to get there.

TRY NEW THINGS

You never know who or what you'll attract when you're willing to try new things. My husband loves cycling, but when we met, I had no desire to get on a bike and said no emphatically if he asked me to go on a ride with him. But then one day, I decided to say yes. I was nervous and scared, but I enthusiastically agreed to go with him. "Sure, I'll go with you. That sounds like so much fun!" I went on that first ride and had the best time! He says I became more attractive to him because I was willing to participate in his hobby, and in the end, it was one of the reasons he fell in love with me. And I fell in love with cycling! So there you go. You never know unless you try.

My fear of public speaking held me back in my Broadway career, and I couldn't let myself make the same mistake in my business. I had to become a strong, confident, and inspiring speaker, and share my story to help others, so I said yes to speaking invitations even when the thought of doing so still terrified me. I knew I'd never grow if I didn't conquer my fear.

How did I do that, exactly? Through practice—lots of it! And even though I spoke regularly, my entire body shook, and I was sick to my stomach before, during, and after my first twenty or so presentations. They weren't pretty either. I sucked, and I don't even remember what I said. But I did it, and that was a victory in itself.

HAVE A MANTRA

The power of positive self-affirmation always helps me get past my fears. It sounds hokey, but trust me, it really works. It's like Amy Cuddy's Wonder Woman pose. Before going into a meeting, making a sales pitch, or taking on anything that can impact your business, be positive. Take your confidence to the next level. Say, "I'm smart. I have something they want. I'm an amazing person, and they want to work with me." I say these things to myself constantly!

Instead of asking people to try your product or to join your team, say with certainty, "I'm doing big things with this." Tell them that you are growing personally, that you're on an incredible team, and that you are so excited and haven't been happier in years! Do it with enthusiasm. Avoid using the words "probably" and "try"—they have no place in your business vocabulary. Go out and boldly tell the world that you are a successful entrepreneur and that they need you in their life!

DRESS TO IMPRESS YOUR EX

My mother is a beautiful woman inside and out. She is an extremely passionate person and always tells it like it is (the good, bad, and the ugly). She cuts right to the chase, and she sugarcoats nothing. When she speaks to you in her adorable Russian accent and tells you what she thinks, you listen. Once, when I was around seventeen, I was dressed like a bit of a slob (I mean, it was the nineties), and I told my mom I was heading out to run an errand and was sure not to run into anyone.

My mom said, "Don't ever think like that! Every time I go out hoping I won't run into someone I know, I always do. Then I wish I had dressed up. Mimi, every time you go out in public, you have to dress like you're going to run into your ex-boyfriend or someone you want to impress." Her words resonated with me, and I pictured myself running into the captain of the football team while wearing sweats and being pimple-faced with no makeup on.

You only have one chance to make a first impression, and

I definitely applied the lesson I learned from my mom to my professional life and career. When I was auditioning, my look was everything! When I was in real estate, I had to always look my best because I had one shot to prove myself to new clients. As an entrepreneur, remember, you are always representing yourself and your future business, even when you aren't technically working. You never know when you will run into someone amazing. You have to wake up every day and remember, "I am my brand, and I have to represent it well. It's okay for me to leave the house in yoga pants, but they should be nice and clean yoga pants." I'm not saying that you always have to buy the high-end brand or be dolled up—just make sure those yoga pants are good quality and look nice on you.

Self-care is a necessity. Your hair, your face, and your skin should also look their best when you leave the house. Take that extra minute to throw on a little tinted moisturizer, mascara, and lip gloss! A girl always feels better when she has a glow on. And here's a bonus: when you look nice and feel good, it's easy to be the best version of yourself. It's easier to smile and look people in the eye and be authentic, genuine, and awesome. You can be bold because you feel confident. You don't have that voice in the back of your head saying, "Oh, man. I wish I didn't look like this right now. I can't network looking like this!"

CONFIDENCE SHINES FROM WITHIN

Your health is one of the most important aspects of how you represent yourself. I don't just mean physical heath—I mean mental health also. As you build your business, you have to keep your health in check. Good health sparks a chain reaction, so taking care of your health increases your confidence, which then grows your business. If you work out a few times a week and you're practicing healthy habits, you flood your mind with good endorphins and serotonin. This causes feelings of happiness to increase, and you'll keep feeling better and better about yourself.

If you're healthy, you look good and feel good. When I think back to a few seasons of life when I wasn't working out and was eating anything and everything, I recall not being in the best mental state. Taking care of yourself helps you remain clearheaded and make better choices. Besides that, you look better physically. Your clothes fit well. You're a little slimmer and tighter; maybe you're more muscular. But most of all, you have the energy you need to build your business and make your dreams come true!

I'm sure either you or someone you know went through an awkward stage while growing up. I know I did! I was an adorable little girl, but between the ages of twelve and sixteen, I was totally gawky, pimple-faced, and flat as a board. I also had to wear braces for way too long. I will never forget in eighth grade (oh god, how I hated that year) I heard a rumor that some of the boys at school had elected me president of the "itty bitty titty committee." *Isn't that terrible?* I was mortified and desperate for my mosquito bites to grow into juicy oranges. But by age sixteen, the braces were off, I had filled out, grown five inches, and finally looked more like a normal person. Heck, I was thin, I was attractive, and most importantly, I was confident, and I began to shine.

REDISCOVERING MY CONFIDENCE

I know I make it sound like I've always excelled at taking care of my appearance, but that certainly isn't the case! When I was in my twenties, I worked out, I danced, and I was very healthy. I lived in Manhattan, kept up with all the latest trends, and I could always pull off whatever I wanted to wear. Then I got pregnant. I was starving all the time. I ate pizza every day, took taxis instead of walking, and in the end, I gained over fifty pounds! And my skin looked terrible again. As most new moms can attest, I lost myself, and self-care went out the window after the baby came. I had completely lost my confidence again.

I spent almost a year carrying around an excess of twenty pounds. Spanx underwear became my best friend, and when I went out, I layered on *two* pairs to make myself feel better. I was in the process of starting my new business at that time, and I remember thinking, "I'm not going out. I don't want to meet people." I realized there was no point in pursuing this opportunity if I didn't do something to change.

As my first step, I stopped ordering pizza every other day. For my second step, I clearly established my mission. I wanted to build a big business and grow a huge organization, but I hadn't been reaching out to the crème de la crème of people I knew because I didn't feel worthy or confident. I needed to get ready to start talking to them.

Second, I started moving. When I lived in Manhattan, I had to walk everywhere, but after I moved to the burbs in New Jersey, the only walking I did was through the garage to get to my car. It didn't take long for me to pack on the pounds after that, so I began walking again. Physical activity is an important aspect of taking care of your health, so you should fit in walks when you can, especially if you don't have time to work out. Walk to a neighbor's house or park in a back spot in a parking lot. Walk to the corner store even if it is a mile away, and opt to walk rather than drive when you have the option. Take care of yourself physically by going for walks or taking a group exercise class with a friend. These minor changes will help you look and feel better! It will also help you with a positive mindset, which is number one when building your own business.

My third step was getting input from others about what I could do to update my look. I asked my sister, who is five years younger than me, to sort through my wardrobe and take me shopping. After she looked at my clothes, she told me that most of what I had was no longer in fashion. *Sigh.* I was definitely out of touch with the fashion trends, the opposite of what I was prior to maternity clothes and motherhood. I also went up a size even though I had lost most of the weight after having the baby, and I had trouble accepting that. People don't tell you how much your body will change after a baby! Most of what I had no longer fit me, and I finally decided to buy new clothes because I couldn't keep trying to squeeze into the old ones. I was sick of looking like a stuffed sausage—enough was enough. If your body changed after you had a baby, or you just aren't the same size you were last year, let me assure you: it's fine. You're still beautiful. You're just different. That's all! Just because your clothes don't fit like they used to, it's not the end of the world. Again, it's all good. Accept it, move forward, change what you can control, and continue to work on being healthy.

If you are struggling with how to dress, you are in luck, because there are so many resources online these days. You can see what people are wearing and what's trendy. Ask a fashionable friend to help you shop! Find looks you like in magazines or follow bloggers on Instagram for inspiration. You can find your ideal look just about anywhere. It may take some digging, but it's worth it because it will help you visualize what you're shooting for. In the end, it will get you out there, you'll look good, and you can be the best version of yourself.

MIRROR, MIRROR ON THE WALL

If you're serious about taking care of yourself, take a minute and look in the mirror. Do you see anything that doesn't represent the brand you want to create? You can start small, like with your hands and feet. How do your nails look? If you're in the beauty business, or if you work in an industry where people can see your hands often, you want them to look good—flaky, chipped nail polish or chewed-up nails are not acceptable. Think about it. Would you get your hair cut by someone who has an awful haircut from 1985? Would you hire an overweight personal trainer? Would you hire a beauty consultant with unkempt hygiene or a personal shopper wearing mom jeans? No!

Small, realistic changes in your routine can work wonders to build your confidence, which will help grow your business. Wake up ten minutes earlier so you can spray on some dry shampoo and quickly blow dry your hair. Add a little mascara, lip gloss, and bronzer, and you'll be ready to face the world.

ACKNOWLEDGE THE WORK

Once you start looking and feeling better, you'll probably

receive some compliments, and you have to learn how to take them! I remember when I began to lose weight, my skin was improving, and I started to blow out my hair instead of doing the bun-air-dry method. People took notice. They complimented me. When this first started happening, I had some kind of internal defense mechanism that wouldn't let me receive the compliments.

I'd say, "Oh gosh, no I don't," or, "Oh really? No, I don't think so."

Finally, someone said, "Just say, 'Thank you,'" and that really hit me.

I learned that I should acknowledge the effort I put into my appearance and say, "Thank you," when I received a compliment. Over time, I learned that taking a compliment instead of pushing it away is an honest response, and it shows that you are confident and genuine. I highly suggest you start putting this into practice. And on the flip side, you should practice complimenting others on a daily basis. When I say "practice," I mean "give." The more you give, the more you get, and the best version of yourself will continue to shine through!

Chapter Five

LOVERS (AND HATERS)

First dates aren't always great, right? Sometimes you're lucky enough to see those sparks right away—I do believe in love at first sight!—but when you're starting to put yourself out there and build your business, you're going to hit some bumps along the road. Be patient.

In my experience, people often expect instant success. If they get a couple of rejections right off the bat, they want to give up. They have yet to develop a growth mindset, and they'll say, "Well, I guess I'm not good at this. Maybe this isn't for me."

To help get you through your "starting season," which can be rough, I want you to think about this: Just like you have good dates and bad dates, there are going to be lovers and haters in your life.

Remember this when you start your business, and don't let it get you discouraged. Think of it this way: imagine you have a friend who decides to go to beauty school on a whim. She graduates and sends you a text that says, "Hey! I'm so excited! I just graduated from beauty school and wondered if you'd be my first customer? I want to cut and color your hair, and have you model for some photos. I'll give you a discount!" What would you say?

Ninety-nine percent of us would probably decline and come up with an excuse as to why now is not a good time. You'd tell her you just got your hair done, you had a gift certificate to another salon, or just make up any excuse because, let's face it, you love your friend dearly, but she has no experience! You don't want her messing up your precious hair. You might also be wondering if she will really stick with this as a career. If she continues with styling hair and the first few customers look good, then you'd consider letting her cut yours.

I also want you to know that, unfortunately, some of your family and friends will probably be your biggest haters. You need to know this in advance so you won't be surprised when it happens. Most people aren't entrepreneurial by nature and have been taught to think about creating wealth through job security. And honestly, lots of people wish they had the courage to start a business or try something out of the box, so instead of being happy for you and your pursuit, they pooh-pooh it.

Here's a tip: it's not your job to convince them to support you—it's your job to carry on with uber confidence! Let their doubts fuel you to work harder, to prove them wrong, and to smile bigger when your bank account starts to grow.

When you reach out to your mom, grandmother, sister, or best friend, it's likely they may respond with, "I'm not interested," or "Now isn't a good time," or they will come up with an excuse. I'm not saying that all of them will reject your offer, but if they do, I want to assure you that's perfectly normal. Don't respond in a negative manner, don't be discouraged, and most importantly, don't quit! Your family and friends love you, and they assume that you already know you have their undying support. However, you may need to remind them that you need them.

WHAT ABOUT THE NAYSAYERS?

Unfortunately, I've had some negative experiences with a few of the people in my life when I started building my business. I don't think they realized how negative they were being. I was working hard to build something of my own, and I was highly sensitive to their words. I truly believe in my heart they never meant to be hurtful or offensive, but on a few occasions, they really hit me hard. I'm sharing this with you because I want you to know that this might happen, and if it does, you will be okay. I promise.

This journey is emotional and can be mentally taxing. You have to keep other people's words in perspective. The people who shoot you down may be miserable in their own situation or have a dream they didn't pursue, and they are still carrying that baggage years later. Their negativity has everything to do with them and nothing to do with you. Just let it go. You have a long life to live, and you should want to spend it surrounded by positive people. This goes for both your business and personal life!

THE LISTS

I suggest you make two lists when you start building your business. First, make a list of the people you love and who love you. These are the people you would call if you had great news to celebrate or needed help in an emergency. They're there for you no matter what. These are the people you want by your side on this journey.

Second, make a list of the people who do not make you feel good. These are the people who only call you when they have a problem or want to stir up drama. Those are some indicators that they belong on this list. Keep a close eye on this list, and if these people start to cloud your head, remember you wrote their names on this "beware of haters" list, and you expected this from them. Okay?

Another thing you can do is think of the five people you

spend the most time with. Who do you talk to most often? Ask yourself if these are the best people for you to be around. When you start building your business, you will need to get rid of negative people or, at least, take a little hiatus from them in the beginning, even if they are one of your top five. You can't have them wearing you down during this journey. You have to set those people aside and move forward with positive energy. Find people who will be your cheerleaders, and spend more time with people who love and care about you—the ones who seem to be interested in what you're doing and want to help. This is their time to shine, too, so bring them in close!

BREAK UP WITH NEGATIVITY

You have to think of your business as a marriage. If there are people in your life who don't support your spouse, you can't be around them as much. This is the hard part: you have to look at friends and family members from a new angle, and it's disappointing when you discover that certain people aren't positive or supportive. You know in your heart that if they were starting a business, you would encourage them.

You have to break up with negative people just like you would break up with a bad boyfriend. An unsupportive boyfriend shouldn't be a crucial person in your life and neither should an unsupportive friend or family member.

You can start by gradually cutting back on communication with that person. That will create a gentle separation—just like a normal breakup.

We've all been on the receiving end of a break up, so this process should be familiar. Maybe you used to hang out with your boyfriend every weekend, then all of a sudden, he's a little busy. Instead of having dinner together, you grab a quick drink. Work seems to be hectic and taking up more of his time. He says, "Can't today, can't tomorrow. I'm so busy. Sorry." You used to talk on the phone, but now you communicate through text messages.

You have to handle this situation with negative Nancys in a similar way. Slowly reduce communication by rolling that daily phone call back to a weekly one. When they call you, don't answer, and say you are busy over text. Then move on to only texts. If they call you, text them back. If they text you, send them an email a week later. "Sorry, I have been so busy with XYZ and my new business that's taking off." See how they respond. If they respond in a positive way, maybe offering an apology or starting to be more positive and accepting, consider getting close again. If not, then only communicate through email or social media at most. Keep them at a distance. Take time to respond. That is the very last step before a complete cut off! I know it sounds harsh, but keeping negative people around can and will affect you if you don't cut them off.

Examine your life as the break-up process moves along. Do you seem happier and less stressed? Have they asked you why you've been distant? Do you miss them, or do you actually feel calmer? Are you free from the dread of an uncomfortable encounter or conversation with this person? If so, you're ready to pull back on the texts and move into contact only through social media.

Do not feel bad about your break up with negativity. There's nothing wrong with doing what's healthy and best for yourself. If this person asks, "Is everything okay?" you don't need to come up with an extravagant explanation. You've seen this person's true colors. If they figure it out and say something like, "I know I haven't been a good friend to you. I'm sorry, and this is why," then maybe you can bring them in a little closer. However, in my experience, I've found that it's rare for negative and self-involved people to change.

CREATE NEW CONNECTIONS

Find your positive people. As Mr. Rogers says, "look for the helpers," and in this case, it's important to connect with other business owners as you begin your journey. You need to make as many friends as possible in your own industry, but you also need to network with people who are building successful businesses in other niches. All of these people are great motivators. You can learn so much from them, and they will be a positive influence. Over the years, I've connected with so many incredible and inspiring entrepreneurs, both in network marketing and in other spaces ranging from retail owners to online entrepreneurs and anyone in between. Connecting with them has been tremendously helpful in giving me a perspective of short- and long-term success. We've all helped each other out at one time or another, and we give one another valuable advice.

The more people in your network that you have befriended, been kind to, or strategized with during ups and downs, the more people you can count on who truly understand business ownership. When something isn't going well in your business and you reach out to a friend or family member, you might get advice like, "Well, you should just quit," or, "Maybe this isn't the right thing for you." You won't get such a response from another entrepreneur. They know that success takes time. They know that failure is a part of success. It's important to find mentors to help you navigate through tough times, share their experiences, and give you fresh perspectives.

DOS AND DON'TS

Here's a handy list of dos and don'ts as you assess your relationships.

DOS

- **Reach out beyond family and friends.** Don't try to build your business by only asking and expecting your friends and family to buy from you.
- **Add value.** Show people you have something to give, that you are finding success, and you know what you're doing.
- **Break up.** Some friends may be haters—either right at the beginning or over time. They might be jealous of your success or your courage, and that's their private issue. If they have regrets about their own unfulfilled dreams, don't take those on. Break up with the negative people in your life.
- **Leverage successful people.** Ask people who are more successful than you for advice.
- **Branch out.** You will get nuggets of wisdom from all of them, and you'll become wiser over time. And you never know where these conversations might take you! That successful person might buy from you, become a referral source, or even join your team. Successful people gravitate toward other successful people, and they're always looking to have their hands in different pots to diversify their income.

DON'TS

- **Don't be afraid!** Go out with no agenda and talk with successful people. Chances are, they did the same in the past, and now it's their turn to give advice. Trust me. Successful people love helping others.

- **Don't write people off.** This applies to haters, too! Some friends may not realize how they come across. Half of the time, it's a fluke, so don't be too sensitive about words that rubbed you the wrong way. Keep building and keep doing you!

- **Don't let "no" get you down.** As you build your business, share your product, and look for people to join you, some will say no. That's okay! The word "no" is not always their final answer. Circumstances change. A friend once told me, "It's not how you treat the yeses; it's how you treat the nos that dictates your success." In my experience, I've found this to be true. I've seen many initial nos turn into yeses. Former nos have become customers, consultants on my team, and referral sources who have helped with my business. "No" really means, "Not right now." Don't let an initial rejection get you down. Keep pressing on!

PART II

Play the Dating Game

Chapter Six

SPREAD A LITTLE
LOVE EVERY DAY

I'll never forget the moment I received my starter package for my new business. I was told that I should share my new, exciting business with my friends and family, so I did just that. I put together a list of about fifty people, crafted my announcement email, held my breath, and hit send! With butterflies in my belly, I constantly checked my email, waiting for responses like, "Congrats!" and, "I want to buy what you're selling," or, "This sounds amazing," etc. I figured for sure I would get five or ten clients right away! Instead, I got one response three days later that didn't even end in a sale. I was crushed. I was so excited, I put myself out there, and one person responded. My heart sank; it felt like it was in my stomach. I remember thinking, "Oh, shit. This is going to be harder than I thought." And honestly, I wanted to throw in the towel then and there.

It was tough for me to wrap my head around what was happening. I came from real estate, which was a world of instant gratification. If I wanted to find new customers, I typed an ad, posted it on Craigslist, and waited for the phone calls to roll in. In fact, I was usually so inundated with interest I could barely keep up with demand. I felt like I had been sucker punched during the first few weeks of my new endeavor, but I decided to keep going. I continued reaching out to people, and crickets continued to chirp in response. I kept reminding myself that I knew people who had been successful in network marketing. It was possible. I just needed more time.

DITCH THE BLAST APPROACH

I was educated, hungry for success, and ready to hustle. I appreciated that this was going to be hard work, but so far, I wasn't getting anywhere. After a lot of nos and attempts to network and sell through social media messages, emails, and texts, I said to myself, "I have to figure this out. What am I doing wrong?" So I began to dig for expertise: I read books on the industry and listened to CDs, watched videos, and read any blog I could get my eyes on from other entrepreneurs and experts in the field.

During this self-development period, I learned one of the

most important lessons of how to build this business in the most effective way possible—one person at a time. Instead of blasting everyone with copy-and-paste messages, I needed to focus on spending time and having human conversations with people. Two hours with one person would be more valuable than attending a networking event and having five-minute conversations with twenty different people. It was about standing out, making connections, and getting to really know someone rather than exchanging business cards and forgetting the face to the name after one cocktail!

I made two goals: (1) instead of messaging hundreds of people and posting ads, I tried to simply connect with one new person each day and (2) add value to someone every day—find one point of connection and go from there.

NATURAL GROWTH

Over the next few months, as I started to build my business and talk to new people, I realized the less I made it about me, the more traction I gained. We tend to talk about ourselves a lot and revert conversations back to our own experiences. We make too many "I" statements instead of asking about the lives of others. When we ask questions, those types of conversations create a natural "in" for your product or service and help you find out if you can truly help the person you are talking to. Show authentic interest in their why. When you stop looking for how people can help you and start searching for how you can be of service, everything changes.

Goodness naturally flows from you when you have a genuine interest in other people's lives and what they're doing. When you make the effort to be the caring and loving person that you'd want to do business with, you sprinkle that goodness on people. Start taking this approach, and I promise that your friendships and your business will grow!

When I was at a workout class with my one-year-old son, a new mom was there with a baby who was just a few months old. It was her first time working out since giving birth, and after we did a swift loop around the block with our strollers, she was red, hot, clearly exhausted, and about to throw up on a bench.

I walked over to her and said, "It's okay. I felt the same way when I first started." She caught her breath, and I ran the next loop right next to her, making sure she was okay. She was a little embarrassed, but I made a new friend that day. We connected on social media, and she shared that she was desperately looking to work from home, as she was laid off during pregnancy. She ended up joining my business, and I don't think that would have happened if I hadn't empathized with her during her rough day.

When I decided to talk to this woman, I didn't have an

ulterior motive—I just put myself out there as the person I wanted to be. Just being a nice human. When you take the agenda out of your interactions and make others feel good for no reason in particular, it sets you apart. In the back of every businessperson's mind, there's always the thought of what you might gain from someone, but personal benefit shouldn't be the driving force behind anything you do.

In business, the bottom line in terms of big money and success is whether or not people find you valuable. The number of people you touch is the determining factor in the amount of money you will make. Meet as many people as possible and maximize your best self. The number of people you are genuinely good to, the more they will want to help you be successful. Your goal is to create a valuable interaction with every person you meet and make their day a little better. That is what builds your business.

Once I made this discovery, "connection" became my mantra. I was all in! Whether I was going for a walk or going to the store, I was connecting. I treated everyone the same, no matter who they were to me. It took practice, but it became second nature for me to share what I do and to talk about my goals and plans.

You can easily do this, too. Get a phone number, then follow up with an invitation for coffee, a drink, or a workout class. Take the time to get to know people. It's like a game of tennis: you ask a question, and they ask a question. You ask a question, and they ask a question. You give a compliment, and they feel more relaxed and trusting. The more questions you ask, the more others will ask you in return. People who take a true interest in other people are the ones who get ahead. We all know people like this, and we also know people who interrupt you to tell their own story and barely let you get a word in. These are the people who roam around talking about themselves, trying to top you with every story, leaving you thinking, "Oh my God, I cannot stand this person for one more second!"

Instead of saying, "Hey, I want to take you out because I'm building my business, and I wonder if you could help me with referrals," say this: "I'm trying to meet people in the area. I'd love to treat you to a coffee and get to know you a little better."

Instead of saying, "You have been so successful in your career! I think you should join my team because you would kill it!" say this: "Hey, I really admire what you have done in your career. I am starting to build my own business, too, and would love to pick your brain. Could I treat you to a coffee next week? It would mean the world to me!"

As you become more comfortable, people will become more intrigued by what you're doing because you didn't push it on them. However, when you meet, you do want to let them know what you're doing. Wrap up the visit with something like, "So if you know someone who might be interested or could benefit from this, I'd love it if you could connect me with them. No pressure." Then you grab their coffee and pay for it because it's a kind, memorable gesture.

TRUE ENGAGEMENT

Once you start meeting people and making real connections, you become memorable. Even if someone barely knows you, they can say, "She's so nice. I met her at a party, and she was cool." When it comes to connections, you want to emphasize quality over quantity. You can't treat networking like your wedding day, where you spend time hugging and kissing everyone in brief encounters. The "Thanks so much for coming!" approach won't build real relationships. Spend your time having meaningful conversations rather than working a room and shaking hands all over the place. Strive for authenticity.

Also, put your phone away when you talk to people. Some people are so attached to their phones, it's killing them socially, and it's killing their business. Sometimes when I have dinner with friends, they text the entire time or scroll their social media accounts. I'm thinking, "Are you kidding me? Can't we just have dinner?" Commit to putting your phone away, and enjoy your time making real connections and looking people in their eyes.

When you truly engage with people, it takes the pressure off—you feel cool, easy, and stress free. After I launched my business, my husband said, "We're going to meet some of my coworkers for drinks. He knew I was struggling and wanted to help. "Mir, make sure you bring some samples, and go meet some new people." The thought of doing this made me nauseous, but I knew he was right, and decided to go for it. I packed three samples in my purse, I went out feeling good, and I discovered it was fun and easy to make new friends! As I started to talk with people, the connections just happened naturally; I didn't try to push anything. Instead of talking about my products and what I do, I shared personal stories, talked about real life, and asked questions to get to know people better. Then I listened to their stories in return. No agenda. It was actually fun. My business did come up in one conversation, and I shared a sample! I also made two great connections that night and planned to follow up afterward.

MAKE NEW FRIENDS

It doesn't matter if you own a restaurant, salon, or an online business—it won't succeed if it's only built on the support of friends and family. As wonderful as it is to have them in your corner, you have to expand your network early on. Someone once said to me, "Your network equals your net worth." I take that seriously. If you have one hundred people in your network, reach out to all of them, and they all say no, you end up with zero business. You need a bigger network, and you need to constantly grow it! You have to meet new people every day and reconnect with the ones you know in person, on the phone, and on social media.

At the end of the day, my goal is to make as many friends as possible. Nowadays, with social media, you can connect with anyone, and you can easily expand your network. After you talk with someone, say, "It was great chatting with you. Are you on any social media? Facebook? Instagram? I'd love to connect and see more pictures of your kids!" *Boom!* Just like that, you're connected.

The key to connecting with others is simple. Be present in the moment. Once you've decided to do that, be the initiator—the one who creates conversation. Be energetic and keep your phone in your bag.

Be the girl you want to be. If you're shy, you can break out of it one step at a time. Give someone a compliment. Ask a question. Practice in front of a mirror. The more you do it, the easier it becomes, and the results will surprise you. And remember, compliments are the easiest in. They invite others to relax, and they begin to trust you because you make the conversation about them, not you.

COFFEE ANYONE?

Meeting people at your job is another way to build your network. If you work at a large company, or if you work with a lot of people, you can't go to lunch with your two best friends every day. Stroll around, meet someone new, and extend an invitation to grab a coffee during the midday lull. Use your full-time job to network with coworkers and other colleagues. Their networks are full of lots of people you don't know. That is how you build a big business!

GET SOCIAL

There is a misconception that real relationships can't be built on social media, but I've found the opposite to be true. People actually tend to open up more when they're typing online and not staring you in the face.

One way to connect with others on social media is to leave sincere comments rather than just hitting the Like button. Wish people a happy birthday, send condolences, and comment on milestones. Once you've made that connection, take the conversation a step further and engage through direct messages. Compliment, ask questions, stay engaged. Share your business. Repeat.

You can also meet new people through social media by clicking on a friend of yours and taking a look at their friends and who they're following. Find the profiles that look appealing to you; people who are socially active would be great to connect with. It's okay if you don't know them—don't be shy.

Post a sincere comment about a photo and then hit the "Add Friend" or "Follow" button, and if they don't accept your request, it's okay. No harm done. Social networking is one of the easiest ways to grow your audience and reach more people. But don't prejudge either. You can't judge a book by its cover. Don't be shy to comment and compliment. At the end of the day, a compliment can make someone's day! And maybe they come back and then follow *you* or add you as a friend. It's a fun game really, but if you don't play the game, it will be hard to grow your digital business, especially as ecommerce is expanding quickly. Don't overthink. Get on social media for fifteen minutes a day and follow new people, compliment, and connect over and over and over again. Trust me, you will thank me later!

DOS AND DON'TS

DOS

- **Give lots of compliments.**
- **Connect with someone new every single day.**
- **Go out and meet new people.**
- **Invite people out for coffee, cocktails, or get togethers.**
- **Get social on social.**

DON'TS

- **Talk all about yourself only.**

- **Prejudge anyone.**
- **Send cold messages.**
- **Not pay on a first date!**

Years later, I found myself in a Mommy and Me class with my second child and faced another unexpected, emotional moment when the woman sitting next to me started bawling. It turned out it was the anniversary of her mother's death, and it hit her hard. Instead of simply offering her a tissue and giving my condolences, I took an extra step and asked for her phone number. After class, I grabbed lunch from a local cafe, texted to ask for her address, and brought her lunch. She appreciated the gesture, and we're still friends to this day. I wasn't exactly sure what to do in this situation, but I knew I had to do something, and sometimes, that's just what we need to do. Doing something is better than doing nothing at all.

I don't tell this story to portray myself as a saint. I'm far from perfect. Sometimes, I even forget family members' birthdays. I am human. We all make mistakes, but at the end of the day, every interaction we have can make someone's life better! And it will make your life better, too. It takes deliberate attention to your surroundings and practice, but eventually it will become second nature to you. The more people you impact, the happier you will be. When you focus on how you can better someone's day, with no ulterior motive, success and new relationships will follow.

So put your phone down and embrace the world. Good karma will return to your business and personal life!

DON'T BE A STRANGER

I had a pretty rough couple of years not too long ago. I had to repair a pregnancy hernia, suffered a miscarriage, broke my ankle, and then when I finally got pregnant, I developed chronic pain in my hips and feet. It was probably the hardest time in my life to date. To this day, I still remember the people who called or sent a card to say they were thinking of me. I also remember the people who didn't. It doesn't take much to make a phone call, and a little bit goes a long way.

Find small, meaningful ways to reach out. For example, it seems that friends, family, business associates, and acquaintances all host fundraisers on social media, and that's wonderful. You can be the person who regularly donates to these campaigns, even if it's just a small amount, like ten dollars. Why should you do this? First, it's a tax write-off; and second, it will make a memorable impact in someone's life. Plus, you'll feel good about what you did with that ten dollars—probably better than you would if you had spent it on a couple of lattes. You could give up those coffees and use the money to make someone's day instead!

Look for everyday opportunities to be the change, and it will begin to come naturally. Over time, your personal brand will evolve, and people will think, "Oh, she's such a nice person," not, "She's that person who just tries to get me to buy her product." Remember, there can be no hidden agenda behind your gestures.

ASSUME THE BEST

When it comes to business and personal relationships, you have to assume the best and not the worst. I coach people who get frustrated when potential clients don't call them back after a few days. Don't get hung up on that. You have to assume she has a lot on her plate, or maybe she's in bed with the flu. She's not a terrible person who has a grudge against you!

When we assume the worst, our imaginations tend to run wild, and we get worked up over the smallest things. When you give people the benefit of the doubt, life gets easier. You are less fussy about details, and you free yourself from unnecessary stress and grief. I mean who needs that!

When you lead with a positive mindset and assume the best, you begin to transform from the inside out. You actually become happier. Once, a friend told me she was angry with another friend because she didn't call her on her birthday until 10 p.m. She said, "I can't believe she forgot my birthday!" I thought this was a negative way to view her friend's gesture. Instead, she could have said, "I'm so happy my friend remembered to call me on my birthday. We're all so busy, and she took the time to call." I mean that friend could have been sick or going through a crazy workday or—*gasp*—she forgot and remembered at 9:55 p.m. to call! *Who cares?* You have the power to shape events and give them a positive spin. When you do that, your life becomes much brighter.

Lastly, give people grace. Everyone is living life and doing the best they can. Newsflash: it's not always about you! Go out in the world and become a positive influence for others and brighten their days. Believe me, it will serve you in your health, your relationships, your business, and every aspect of your life five times over.

Chapter Seven

PLAY THE FIELD

Just like in Dating 101, one of the biggest rules when building your network marketing business is: keep your options open.

You have to prospect new people all the time. No matter what type of business you're in, and especially if you're in network marketing, you have to play the game—the numbers game, that is. You build your business and your client base by prospecting over and over again. The more people you connect with, the more successful you will be.

If you want to start strong in your prospecting game, you have to let go of everything you've been (and done) in the past. If you were overweight and had acne in high school, forget about that. If you were a complete jerk in college, or at some other point in your life, leave that behind. Make today a new beginning and just talk with people. Reach out as the best version of yourself, be authentic, and keep fear and emotion out of the process.

Let's say you're single, and you're an elementary school teacher. You are on the hunt to find yourself a hubby, but all of your coworkers are married women. So how will you meet someone? You have to get out there and date! You need to attend events and go to various places where men (or women) hang out, ask friends to introduce you, go online, go to networking events, or use a dating app. I've personally attended three weddings of couples who met online, because it works! In life and in business, you have to put yourself out there, or you'll never meet new people.

Don't wait until you feel like you're established to go and talk to people. Get out there during your first few days of business. Find people, talk to them, and get to know their hearts and minds. Get to know their vision and determine if they'd be a good fit for you and if they could benefit from a side income or complete career change. Maybe they have an entrepreneurial spirit. If not, they might be interested in trying one of your products or services. Or maybe they become a new friend, and that's awesome, too! Because friends have friends, and referrals are a huge part of the business world. Do what you need to do to meet people. Don't sit at home, pouting and wondering why your business isn't growing. Get out there and build it!

THE WORLD IS YOUR OYSTER

If you're on the dating scene and go to the same bar every Friday night, with the same group of friends, chances are you probably won't meet anyone new. The same goes for building your business: to truly expand your network, you'll need to deviate from your normal routine. Take that yoga class, go to that wine tasting, or attend that sporting event. Go somewhere you've never gone before and spend time with new and old friends. You never know who you will meet or click with in a new way!

Be that girl who reconnects with old friends. Use social media to contact them, and then meet face-to-face if possible. Get conversations going. Put coffee or drinks on the calendar, and then put yourself out there again and again. If you're friendly, excited, and reconnect in a genuine way, people will appreciate that. As you talk to old friends, it's inevitable that your business will come up in conversations.

DON'T SETTLE DOWN TOO EARLY

As your team grows, your responsibilities as a leader increase. This can be a tough balance to strike, but it's vitally important to continue working on new business, even when you're being pulled in a million other directions. The good news is that the clients and partners who will stick with you—the real hustlers, dreamers, and players—won't need much hand-holding. Find them, enroll them, train them, and cast the vision. Then continue to prospect.

Continue talking with as many people as possible. Be cool and always be leading by example and continue to grow your own business first. You don't know if the amazing person you've found is going to stick around or whether or not the situation is going to play out the way you think it will. Play the field.

Sometimes, a consultant enrolls a new person on their team who says all the right things, and boom, they think they have found "the one." But when building your network marketing business, you can't throw all of your eggs into one basket. The same goes for hiring new employees or adding new customers. It's easy to think that just because you've signed up a big fish, the success will roll in quickly. Unfortunately, that's not usually the case.

You might enroll a new partner onto your team, and while you're helping them along, you think, "This person is it. They're the one. I'm done, I have hit the jackpot, baby!" I want to tell you right now, that is one of the biggest mistakes I see entrepreneurs make. Just because someone is great now, it doesn't necessarily mean they will be a rock star a year from now. Same thing with a boyfriend, right? They are amazing for six months, then all of a sudden, they change. Something happens or they meet someone else and break up with you—after you stopped speaking to all of your friends and family to spend every waking hour with said boyfriend. Then you're left with no one. *Do not be that girl.*

Sometimes, the person who experiences success in the beginning slows down. Or they hang on tight to a few customers or new team members and forget about obtaining new business and networking. You never want to let a new person get a sense of how important they are to your business until they prove themselves first and show up. You never want someone thinking—especially in the beginning—that they can make or break your business. Because one person can never do that! Remember that. New business and new blood are the key to success and longevity.

You have to understand that people change, and all you have control over is what you do. You can share your business, share your products, and develop your mindset. You can't hold on to the same person or be unwilling to part ways if they aren't who you thought they'd be. Don't keep this person on board and keep trying to fix them or to shape them into something they're not. It's tough to predict who will be the best performer, so you have to keep bringing fresh people in!

READ THE SIGNALS

You wouldn't date someone for a week and then think you're

going to marry them, right? And they probably wouldn't think that about you. Right? The same type of thinking applies when seeking prospects for your team—you have to play the dating game. This gives you some leeway if the person doesn't end up being right for your business, and it motivates them to work harder to create a partnership with you.

Let's say someone is interested in working with you, so you set up a phone call with them for training. The person seems great, so you set up a second call, but they miss it. They text you later that they got busy and forgot. *Ding! Ding! Ding!* That's your first sign that this person may not be a good fit. It's possible they might be worth another shot, but a miss like that is equivalent to a guy standing you up on a Friday night.

As women, we're upset by these disappointments, but then we come running back. We think, "It's okay! No worries." We start getting into desperation mode because we think we *need* this person in our business. Don't do that! Instead, you need to act with confidence. Your time is valuable, and now the ball is in your court. Your mindset should be, "You need to earn back my trust. Next time, it's not going to be that easy to make an appointment with me, and I will give you some homework first. I'll forgive you, I will give you a second chance, but I'm not going to make it as easy. You'll have to work around my schedule, and earn back my trust."

Keep the situation balanced and in check. Do what you'd do if your boyfriend ditched you and tried to make plans again.

PLAY HARD TO GET

Let's say you go out on an amazing first date with someone. As soon as you get home, you text the guy and say, "That was amazing. Can we go out again tomorrow? Are you my boyfriend now? What's our status?" Do you think he'll want to go out with you again? Probably not.

When you're prospecting, you can't give off the vibe that you're desperate. You are not totally available! Talk with people and set up appointments. Don't give them your whole presentation up front. Don't say, "I'm building a business. If you join me, you can make a ton of money. Are you in?" That's lame and impersonal and will immediately turn them off.

Be cool. Wait a day or two to reach out again after that first meeting. Say, "It was so great chatting with you. I had such a nice time getting to know you. I know we talked a bit about my business, but we didn't really go into detail. I'd love to tell you more about it." Phrase it however you want, but be cool, not desperate.

And when you're dating and that guy finally reaches out and asks, "Hey, are you free next week?" you don't want to respond with, "Yeah! I'm free Monday, Tuesday, Wednesday, Thursday, and Friday. I'm free all day, every day. I'm yours. You tell me where to be, and I'll be there!" You need to sound professional and give off the vibe that you are successful and busy even if you're new at this. You want to exude that success and be confident. People consciously and subconsciously don't want someone whose schedule is wide open. They want to eat at a restaurant that has a waiting list, and they want to visit a doctor who is slammed with appointments. If a restaurant is empty or a doctor has no patients during the day, it raises a lot of questions.

Setting appointments shows people you are busy. In business and in dating, being busy is sexy, attractive, and desirable. People want to know that you're not at home every night. You work, but you have a life, too, and you want to send that vibe when you're talking to new people. When you're prospecting, let people know you're busy but can squeeze them in at this or that time.

You need to present a bit of a challenge, like the guy you fell hard for in your teens or twenties. He wasn't always available—he was busy. You need to be like him. You have something awesome to offer in your business, and you don't need to chase people down. *You* are the heartthrob. You're a busy, successful, leader, and if they want to be a part of what you're doing, they'll need to book time with you.

PLAY IT COOL

I mean be cool, confident, and attractive, without being annoying. Don't stalk people to get them to join your team or buy from you. You want to be smooth like Jennifer Lopez or Beyoncé. Get what I mean?

Even if you are still learning about your products or services and you don't know every single detail, speak about them as confidently as possible. Say something like, "I don't exactly know all the details, but I'm really excited about it. I would love for you to give it a try and share your feedback with me." That approach is so much better than saying, "Please buy this from me. Pretty please? Please?" There's more power and influence in phrases like, "I would love your feedback. I really admire you. You're someone I trust, and it would mean a lot if you would support me."

If you want the truth, you most likely won't get many supporters right away. It will take time. Most people by nature are either envious or wary of your willingness to try something new, or they just don't understand why you feel the need to add something more to your plate. Trust me, people are watching, and they're waiting for you to prove yourself.

If your message is, "Join my team. Buy my products. Make me money!" it will give you a bad reputation quickly. It harms the industry's reputation, too. People will think, "All these consultants do is hound people!" The best tip I can give you is not to spill the beans right away. Give people a teaser, and make them want to come back for more. If someone asks a question about your business, answer it quickly, and then switch the topic right back to them. If they're interested, they will prompt you for more details. And if they aren't, you avoid dumping information on an uninterested party. The key is to let the other person do most of the talking so you can find out what kind of person they really are and determine whether or not the opportunity is right for them.

If you dominate conversations or say the same things over and over, you'll miss important cues. If you're committed to listening, you'll get a better sense of people's motivations. There are many different reasons why people might want to join you. It's not always about money, so hear them out, and treat everyone the way you would want to be treated.

FIND WHAT'S MISSING

Never judge a book by its cover, and never assume that you know what's happening in another person's life. Don't rule anyone out as a prospect because of what's on the surface. Maybe that beautiful, successful accountant, lawyer, doctor, or realtor who has a perfect life on social media hates their job and is hiding their real story. A stay-at-home mom who lives in luxury because her husband makes a ton of money might be miserable, and maybe she needs a new venture in her life. Or a teacher or social worker who loves their job is looking for a way to make more money to pay down their student loans.

You don't know what's going on behind closed doors or between another person's ears. There could be something in their professional life, friendships, or marriage that leaves them wanting more. I'd have to write another book to tell you all of the different reasons why people have joined my team, but for now, I can tell you that money was not the primary factor for most of them. Many people came from unexpected places, at unexpected times, and I never would have found them if I hadn't played the field.

IDENTIFY THE WHY

When you're prospecting, remember to treat everyone equally. Everyone has a why or something that is missing, but it's not written on their foreheads. You have to find out their reason why or what is motivating them. You don't know what's happening in anyone else's life, so they all have an equal possibility of needing your product or service. Don't rob someone of the opportunity because you don't ask or think they won't need it.

Try to figure out what kind of person you're talking to. If you're a bubbly person and you're talking to someone who is a bit shy, try to match their level. Make an educated guess as to how you might need to tailor yourself for this conversation. Think of how you can best connect with this person. To create lasting connections, you'll need to adjust your demeanor for each interaction rather than act the same exact way around everyone.

ONE SIZE DOES NOT FIT ALL

When it comes to your business and building long-term relationships, a one-size-fits-all script won't cut it. For example, teachers, nurses, social workers, or people in a similar line of work probably didn't choose their careers for financial gain. They're most likely passionate about helping people and are already fulfilled by their jobs. When you talk with anyone in these fields, you'll want to adjust your approach—place the emphasis on how what you do helps others. On the other hand, someone in finance or real estate might be interested in residual potential income, and you'd discuss more about what they can earn if they join your business.

Let's get more specific. Say you're going to meet with a business professional who operates with a business mindset. You'd bring your laptop equipped with numbers and projections and tailor your verbiage to match. If you're meeting with a world-traveling millennial in her early twenties who doesn't have kids, you'd tone down the numbers aspect or talk about a retirement option and instead point out how this business might help pay off student loans and build up a nice travel account. Moms would relate to conversations about working around diaper changes or paying a child's college tuition or after-school sports. When discussing your business with others, consider their position and motivation, and then shape your conversation appropriately to them.

DO YOUR RESEARCH

I once reached out to an Ivy League graduate friend I hadn't seen in years, who was super successful in the finance world. I walked in wearing my favorite pair of ripped jeans, beach wavy hair, and a cute flannel. When I laid eyes on her, I saw that she was clad head-to-toe in pearls, J. Crew, and black pumps! In *Sex and the City* terms, she was Charlotte and I was Carrie. I didn't even have my computer or iPad. I just brought a little notebook and some samples with me. This style and approach may have worked with someone else, but it sure didn't work with her! She was ready to talk facts, numbers, and see a PowerPoint or spreadsheet, while I was ready to reminisce about the past and squeeze some business in. I found out the hard way that doing your research prior to meetings is absolutely essential to building a successful business.

Looking back, I still don't know what I was thinking. I knew this girl was conservative, successful, and worked at a top financial institution in Midtown Manhattan, and I should have planned my approach so I could connect with her. I should have worn heels, a nice blouse, and a skirt or black pants. I should have been more put together. She was interested. She had reached out to me after I sent an email marketing newsletter, and I truly feel my first impression wasn't what she had hoped for. Based on my appearance, I painted the picture that this was a carefree side gig, and she was looking to build a legitimate business. She wanted a professional career, one that she could run on her own terms. Which *was* exactly what I had to offer, but I didn't come across that way. *Ughhhhh!* That one still bothers me. Talk about a learning curve. Now when I meet with someone new, I try to look the part and show that I'm serious about my growing business. If it's a stay-at-home mom, I can dress more casual, but if it's someone who works full time and the meeting is during the work week, I have to have my A game on! This doesn't mean I change who I am—I just adapt to the situation.

In this case, I had some big mistakes to analyze. If you find yourself in a situation where your approach didn't result in a sale or a partnership, try and identify the hiccup and figure out what you will change next time.

BE PATIENT

Not everyone will ask what you do right away, and some

may never ask you at all. I've met with some people once or twice, and the topic of careers just didn't come up. That's fine, but you should work on weaving your business into natural conversation. For instance, you can say something like, "That reminds me of when I was at a work retreat and one of my coworkers..." or, "I'm doing well. Definitely busy. I just got off a great work conference call with some of my business partners!" Be creative with natural ways to point to your business (in a non-salesy way) by referencing something you may have just finished or by telling a good story. And we know everyone loves a good story!

Chapter Eight

PRACTICE YOUR MOVES

As a young child, I fell in love with dancing. I wasn't the best in the class by any means, but I was better than average. At age eleven, I auditioned for a serious dance company, and somehow, they let me in! I fell in love with the art, what it did for my body, my mind, and my heart. I continued to dance competitively in high school and won many awards, both as a team and by myself. I also received scholarships to various programs around the country and went on to dance in college.

It wasn't long before I signed with a top talent agency, Clear Talent Group in New York. I was so excited for what the future would bring. Very quickly, I started getting calls about auditions, and I wasn't afraid to jump right in. I didn't always have the best footwork, jumps, or turns, and I wasn't always the best dancer in the room, but I had the hustle and the heart and knew that practice was a vital part of moving up in that world. The best dancers, the ones who made it to Broadway and beyond, were the ones who took the most classes, showed up to practice early, stayed late, and always came prepared. I had to practice longer and harder than anyone else, make sacrifices, and be willing to fail until I succeeded.

The same concept about practice applies in business. It's a rule of success. You have to practice, practice, and then practice some more until you create muscle memory. You need to get to the point where you don't have to strategize the next step—you need to be able to make your move without thinking about it. It should happen automatically because you have done it more times than you can count.

For example, we know the choreography to the "YMCA" song by heart. We know how to sing "Happy Birthday" without grasping for the words. We know the words to that Madonna or Britney song, or to Sir Mix-a-Lot's "Baby Got Back," because we've sung them so many damn times. We've listened to them over and over, and repetition has committed them to the depth of our brain. Researchers say it takes sixty days to form a new habit or a few thousand hours to master a new skill. The key is to just keep at it. Persistence pays off!

SOMETIMES YOU HAVE TO BOMB

I'm sure you've heard the saying, "Most people would rather be at their own funeral than give a eulogy." This described me to a tee when I first started my business—presenting to a crowd was by far my biggest hurdle. However, just sharing my new business with *one* person gave me anxiety! When I talked with someone face-to-face, I would shake, stutter, and feel sick to my stomach. Over the years, I learned that this is totally normal, and it can be conquered if you work hard enough to overcome the fear.

How did I overcome my weakness? Through practice!

It's crazy that I used to be so fearful of public speaking, and I do it all the time now. I've trained thousands of people while onstage at annual company conventions. I can honestly say that I barely get nervous anymore, and it actually gives me a thrill. I might have a little twinge in my belly right before I begin, but it disappears once I get going because I've learned to love it through practice.

Don't get me wrong—I have bombed before. When my early business partners and I gave our first presentation, we thought we were going to share our passion for what we were doing and for our product. But it was just the opposite: all three of us bombed. We were each terrible in our own way. One partner shook while reading directly from note cards, I was a blubbering mess, and the other partner forgot what she was going to say, and we just kept giving each other the OMG look. We were awful simply because it was our first time trying, and we didn't give ourselves enough time to prepare. We thought we could wing it, and we were wrong.

I learned the hard way that you have to be prepared to give a presentation—maybe even overly prepared. It's true that some people can deliver speeches and give toasts with ease, but it's most likely because they are very well rehearsed. They consider what they are going to say in advance, and then they practice it over and over again until it's second nature.

BUILD MUSCLE MEMORY

Experience trumps talent. Period. When building your business, your job is to get out there as much as you possibly can and talk to people about your product, your service, your passion, and your vision. Talk to anyone who will listen, and get really comfortable talking.

The key is to listen first and then talk. People buy from people they like and trust; you need to get to know them. If you ask a lot of questions, they will reciprocate.

In the early days of my business, I posted a few advertisements online to see if I could get some bites. I got so many inquiries it was overwhelming. I had to talk to so many strangers! People from all walks of life called me, and they didn't even know exactly what they were inquiring about.

Posting the ad was a shot in the dark, but it got me on the phone with tons of new people. I asked questions of them and then shared information about my business and products with over fifty strangers within a month's time. It probably would have taken others six months to talk to that many strangers, but I did it in a few weeks. It was a hectic and crazy experience, but it gave me an edge: with each conversation, I got better and better at talking about my business.

The inquiries from strangers also helped me learn a lot in a short amount of time. I learned when it was time to end the conversation, where questions typically came up, and the types of conversations that led to second meetings. With each new experience, I tweaked my presentation a little more.

In addition to the calls, I practiced my presentation skills with my husband. I made flashcards with potential questions and objections. He read them, and then I responded. He gave me feedback (which was difficult to hear sometimes), but I appreciated his support and involvement. I wanted him to understand the job and what I was doing so he could be a positive influence and sounding board as my business grew.

ALL SPEAKING IS PUBLIC SPEAKING

It doesn't really matter how many people you're talking to; you need to step out of your fear and just do it. The longer you wait and the longer the lag time between presentations and networking meetings, the less prepared you'll be. And if you want me to be totally straight with you, you won't do well.

Public speaking doesn't necessarily mean you're giving a speech. You could just be talking to one, two, or three people. When you're in front of a group or onstage, there might be hundreds of people in the room, but you have to act like you're talking to one person. People need to feel like you're just talking to them. Once you gain confidence in a face-to-face setting, you will get stronger and be more prepared to speak in front of a bigger crowd.

Think about preparation and training for speaking like going to the gym—you'll only see results if you exercise on a regular basis. If you only go a couple of times a month, you're going to be in a lot of pain after each workout. Your body will respond with, "What? What are we doing again? This hurts!" But if you go often, your body will adapt: you grow to like it, you start seeing results, and you won't even be sore over time!

Whether you're talking with someone one-on-one or addressing a large group, you have to bring confidence to every setting. To do that, you have to conquer your presentation and focus on telling your story and sharing your why. Don't think of your approach as selling. You're simply sharing your story, product, and an awesome opportunity that could greatly benefit others. Master that story, and guess what? You'll see that your presentation constantly improves, and it will catapult you into the next level of greatness. As you grow as a leader, you will be able to coach others to do this, too.

DON'T GET COMFORTABLE

Sometimes, a person on my team will say, "Oh my God, I'm presenting at a big event next week, and I'm so nervous!"

I'll respond with, "That's because you haven't done this in three months. You're out of practice."

When you haven't presented in a while or practiced in front of a mirror or video camera, it's much harder to get back into the game. Don't let yourself fall out of rhythm. Continue to do what you do all the time, and keep building your business. Don't become complacent and stop because you had a few good months, because once you stop doing what got you there in the first place, you can move backward quickly.

It all goes back to dating. Let's say you've been dating someone for three years, and you think they're the one. Then suddenly, they drop a bomb on you. They say, "I don't think this is going to work out. We need to break up." *Um, what the hell just happened?*

Now, you're single again and it's scary. It's been forever since you've met someone and gone out on a first date. You seriously can't remember how you did it before. You've lost the hang of it because you've been out of the game for a substantial amount of time. The same thing can happen with your business and presentation skills. Keep talking and presenting. Don't get comfortable and don't stop practicing.

START AT HOME

There are many ways you can practice talking to people. Ask friends or trusted relatives who aren't involved in your business to be your guinea pigs. Take advantage of your time with them and tell your story. Honestly, some of the best feedback comes from people who have no idea what you are doing.

As painful as this might be, you can also record yourself on video and watch it to learn about your presentation habits. Do you stand still, or do you move your body? Do you fidget? Are your arms crossed? Do you have a nervous tick? I tried this strategy and noticed the characteristics I needed to change when talking to others. Even though I've improved by leaps and bounds, I still have areas to work on—I'm constantly evolving. I speak with passion, and I've learned to just be myself. This took *years* of practice and study.

LEARN THE WORDS

I believe that the number of times you've done something is much more important than how long you've been doing it. Some people have been in my industry for ten years, and they are less accomplished than others who have been in it for two. Yes, one year is the same length for everyone, but what matters most is what you do with it.

Sometimes, the longer you have done something, the less experience you actually have. You become complacent with a certain level of success, and you don't strive for more. You stop practicing your moves, and you don't grow. If you can be comfortable with being uncomfortable, you'll grow to love it!

Don't stop until you are so comfortable that your presentation feels like singing that familiar song—you can recite every word without thinking about it. If you have to pull out your notes to answer questions to put on a good presentation, you aren't ready. You need to keep practicing. Learn the words to your song, learn the moves to your dance, and lock it deep into your memory. That way, when someone asks about your business or products on the fly, you can answer with complete confidence and passion. Better yet, they will truly believe you are moving into great things!

Chapter Nine

WILL YOU GO OUT WITH ME AGAIN?

Picture this: you go out with a new guy for cocktails on
Friday night. You tell your bestie that you'll text her a code
word if she needs to call and get you out of there, but you
didn't need to send the text because the date was amazing!
Cocktails turned into dinner, the conversation was flowing,
and he walked you to your front door. Then you gave him
a kiss on the cheek and said, "Good night." Perfection! So
what do you do now? You had an incredible first date, and
you want to make sure there's a second one. How do you
do that?

You call your besties and analyze everything. You spend
hours working on a draft of the perfect text, and you wait
for the absolute perfect moment to send it. You think about

how to play the follow-up game and wonder when you'll go out again. You finally text him, and then you wait to see how long it will take before he texts you back. You want to play it cool and make sure your game is on point, but you also don't want to be too nonchalant—you are interested in him, after all! So maybe you wait a few hours. Or a few days.

Recruiting for your business is a lot like dating—you will go on a lot of first dates. You simply have to. When you first begin, you're figuring out what works and what doesn't. You're discovering which strategies get results and which ones fall flat. All of that is fine, but what you can't do is make the same mistakes over and over again. You have to analyze what went wrong and come up with a solid plan for improvement; you can't have a random approach. If you did, I suppose you could get lucky, but you don't want to build a business that way. You want to build it with perseverance, systems, and well-developed methods. You want to master the art of the follow-up.

WAS IT SOMETHING I SAID?

It's important to take the time to find the best prospecting approach that gets you results. For instance, you might find that you have the best results from twenty-minute discussions, not epic two-hour meetings. Or maybe you see better outcomes when you get to know people over time. Or maybe you find that when you meet people for drinks, you tend to have too many (no martinis for me when I am working) and forget all about the business aspect of your meeting.

It's possible you will want to turn your side hustle into a main gig at some point, and that means you will need to create systems. Systems must be easy to follow and easy to duplicate. Just like after a first date, you'll need to figure out how you will analyze meetings. This will help you minimize mistakes going forward and make the most productive use of your time. Use the following "Questions for Reflection" to get started.

QUESTIONS FOR REFLECTION

After you have meetings, phone calls, and other first-time experiences, ask yourself these questions, and jot down your answers:

- What did I do well?
- What did I forget to do?
- What did I wear?
- What did I say?
- What story did I tell?
- How long was I there?
- What was the outcome?
- Where did the meeting take place? (phone, video conference, face-to-face, events, etc.)

These questions will help you clearly see which patterns lead to partnerships and new business, and which ones consistently fail. For me personally, a thirty-minute phone call or meeting is my sweet spot. Not too long, not too short. If I talk with people any longer than that, we might dive in too deep for a first date, and it gives them the impression that I'm not busy. Of course, the time is extended for face-to-face meetings. I spend the first thirty minutes getting to know the person, and I share how my business and products might benefit them for the last fifteen to twenty. Then, I answer their questions and head to the next step. How do I know all of this? Because I track my meetings—and my results! You discover your own ideal patterns if you systematically analyze what you're doing.

Successful people are busy and manage their time wisely. If you want to appear to be successful, you'd better act like you're busy. You don't want to be the one still talking while the other person is politely trying to end the meeting. You need to be the one to say, "Okay, wow look at the time. Thank you so much for meeting me. This has been a lot of fun, but I've got another appointment in twenty minutes!" If you're ending a phone call or a date with a new boy (or gal), you want to be the one who has the last word, right? End the meeting when you say you're going to, and end it with a follow-up or action item. Say, "I'm going to send you more information," or, "I'll call you tomorrow at four o'clock since you said that will work well for you."

Figure out your most effective medium for connection. What works best with your personality and preferences? For example, some people on my team are social butterflies, so they're better with face-to-face meetings. Others have a tougher time face-to-face and prefer to talk on the phone or through a video conference. Still others are very detailed and like to plan their responses, so they go back and forth with prospects via email.

Personally, I'm a big proponent of connection through the human voice. If I can't meet someone face-to-face, then talking on the phone or through video is great. If you're building a global business, you can't meet with people in other states or countries, so you'll need an alternative way to connect with them. For this, I suggest Skype, Zoom, FaceTime, or another convenient and effective internet conference method. If you aren't one who likes to be on camera all the time, that's okay. You can turn the camera off and post a fabulous picture of yourself instead. The most important thing is for the other person to hear your voice and your excitement.

SCRAP THE THREE-DAY RULE

I'm sure you're familiar with the three-day rule in dating: you don't call the person you went out with for at least three days. That might work in the dating world, but it won't work in business. When you're trying to build a network, you need to follow up with people within forty-eight hours, and if you can do it within twenty-four, that's even better. If you don't reach out in a timely manner, the other person may lose any initial impression they had of you being a professional. Remember, you are the one being interviewed. Your prospect wants to know what kind of mentor, coworker, salesperson, or partner you will be, and following up shows that you are reliable. You're a person of your word.

I want to be clear that following up does not mean you are being annoying. You might think that if you call, you're just chasing someone, but you aren't. It's not "chasing" if you're reaching out to ask if they have questions. You have to change your perspective about following up and realize you are trying to please others and add value. However, you do want to be careful how you go about it: deliver what you promise in a timely manner, but don't be pushy and don't be too available.

You also want to be respectful of other people's time when they do want to talk with you again. You can prepare someone for the conversation by saying, "I'm going to tell you more about myself, my company, and my products. It will probably take fifteen to twenty minutes. Then if you have questions, you can ask me afterward. Does that sound good?" This is helpful because people know what to expect, and they won't zone out or feel pressed for time. There's nothing worse than being stuck in a meeting or presentation and having no idea when it will end.

Be clear that you're going to follow up with them, and let them know what they can expect. Then do exactly what you said you would do. (Here's an insider tip: if people don't have questions, they're probably not interested.)

MORE THAN ONE TOUCH

Statistics say that it typically takes five to twelve touches to complete a sale. So if an initial meeting is your first touch, you'll most likely need to schedule more meetings and send a few follow-up emails or texts. You'll need to make more of an effort to connect and follow up. If you're going into your second or third meeting, you won't want to leave things too open-ended. Say something like, "Okay, the next step is for us to talk again, and we need to answer your questions. Are you available after work tomorrow?"

When you propose times, think about the ones that will work best for that person. Ideal meeting times will vary based on what they do—stay-at-home moms, freelancers, and full-time workers will all have different schedules. Work to accommodate them by offering a couple of open times that will work for them, but don't be incessantly available.

Remember, you have to play the dating game from the beginning. Never make your schedule or your conversation open-ended. A meeting that ends with you saying, "Okay, I'm going to send you an email. If you have questions, let me know," doesn't have any action behind it. Never ever say "Let me know." You are leaving the ball in their court, which is a huge no-no. Instead say, "The email that I'm going to send you will likely leave you with some questions. I know you're probably just as busy as I am, so let's make an appointment now for when we can talk again. How does Friday at noon work for you?"

SCRIPT YOUR SCENARIOS

Prepare for various conversations and scenarios so you're not thinking off the cuff. I suggest creating mini scripts and templates. Here are a few to get you started:

1. When a prospect says, "Hey, I got your email. Great meeting you," you say, "Great meeting you, too. I'll reach out to you on Monday morning to see what you thought and answer any questions." Don't leave the ball in their court—the key here is for you to be in control.

2. When a prospect says, "I'm really interested, but I still have to think about it," you say, "Awesome! I agree it's smart to think about it. I'll reach out to you on Monday morning and see what you're thinking. Be ready with any questions you have for me." Keep the ball in your court—the key here is to agree. Don't fight them. Don't say, "There's nothing to think about. This is the best thing ever. You have to do it." That sends a super shady vibe and makes people nervous!

3. When a prospect says, "Hey, thanks so much, but I'm not interested," you say, "Thank you so much for your time. I totally understand this is not for everyone and the timing might just not be right. But my business grows on referrals, and I truly love helping others, and I am so passionate about what I do. If I send you something and you send it to someone else who is interested, here's how it benefits you..." Ask them, "Would you mind sharing this video, email, or link with your friends or anyone who this might be a fit for, or with others who you think might be interested? I would do X for you." The key here is turning "no" into an opportunity.

Maybe that person is a no-go at the moment, but you can offer them a gift card, free products, or something else of value for a referral. You'll hear "no" a lot, and some people won't respond at all. Don't take this personally.

Don't get mad or upset when people say no, or assume that it will be their answer forever. You can use nos to your advantage by asking them a few questions. Say, "What is it that makes you not interested? I'm just curious. What is it that turns you off to this idea?" Then maybe you can figure out if you made a misstep or whether or not the person has made assumptions or been misinformed. Finally, agree with your nos. Say, "Okay, I totally get where you're coming from. Maybe now is not the time, but I'd love to follow back up with you."

You'll need a system of responses and follow-up schedules. If you don't, you will intend to do it, life will happen, and follow-ups will drag out past forty-eight hours. You might even stop following up after the first or second visit. Maybe your system will be that you reach out two weeks after the second meeting. That's fine. Whatever system works for you is great as long as it's set and you can stick with it. If you drop off the map and fail to follow up, people will think you aren't interested in them. If you're interested, you have to keep reaching out.

EASY CONNECTIONS

These days, with social media, it's so easy to grab someone's social handle for Facebook, Instagram, or LinkedIn and "friend" them. Adding prospects to your social media accounts keeps you connected to them, and it also helps them keep up with what you're doing since you'll pop up on their feed every once in a while.

Earlier in the chapter, I told you it takes about five to twelve touches to complete a sale, so the sooner you follow up, the sooner you'll get those touches. If you are on touch number five and you feel like you're getting nowhere, don't be discouraged; it's normal to not have closed by then. People need time to decide, or timing can be a factor.

Do what you can to keep in touch with others. You can do

that through a newsletter, holiday cards, or summer visits. You never know when someone's situation will change, so you want to design a clear-cut system to keep track of your prospects.

Time is money—don't waste either one with a weak follow-up game. Let your actions show your interest, and chances are you'll get that second date!

A SECOND GLANCE

One of the biggest mistakes business owners make is dismissing people based on first impressions or false perceptions.

That's what happened with me and my husband, Randy. We met during my first week at Skidmore College. I was definitely attracted to him when I saw him at a party, but when we started dating a few years later, I honestly never thought he was the man I would later marry. We came from very different backgrounds and upbringings: him, a Philadelphia city boy, and me, a suburban Jersey girl.

My parents were strict—I was a first-generation American. The importance of education was embedded in me from a young age. I wanted to make my parents proud, so I always did well in school, took AP classes, and most days, I worked my butt off studying. Then I went to a top liberal arts college, worked hard, and got good grades all over again so I could get a great job and live the American dream. My entire life, I had pictured myself marrying someone like me: a Jewish man who was born and raised in the suburbs with a backyard and lived a similar lifestyle. My husband, Randy, was not that guy, but in the end, he was the perfect person for me.

Randy was a rough-around-the-edges city boy who was raised in one of the tougher neighborhoods in Philadelphia. His parents, both academics and social justice advocates, also stressed the importance of education. We had different political, economic, and social opinions and didn't see eye to eye on a lot, but we had *fun* together and great conversations. As we got to know one another, I found out he had a warm, snuggly heart. He was tough on the outside but total mush on the inside. When we first met, he was almost intimidating to me. He wasn't like the guys I typically dated, and I honestly thought he was going to be a fling—not a husband!

I had a perception of my now husband based on the first few times we had met, but when I really got to know him, I found out he was different than what I had originally thought. If I'd gone with my initial perception of him, I would have missed out on a wonderful man. Sometimes, what you're looking for is right in front of you—it just doesn't look like what you expected.

My husband and I are opposites in a lot of ways, but over time, we've become more similar and bring out the best in each other. We make an amazing team and are true partners. The point is, I took a lesson from Dating 101: don't judge a book by its cover. Or in this day and age, don't judge a person by their photos or their descriptions online! Someone with the best résumé who may have been a major success in the past and talks a big game may not necessarily be right for your business. And may not be the best business partner for you! The opposite goes for someone who doesn't look the part. Maybe they don't have the perfect background, current skills, or personality. Maybe they don't have the money to get started right away. It doesn't matter. They might be exactly who you're looking for and might become the top producer on your team. You won't know until you really get to know them and their potential.

We all have a vision of a perfect dream partner, and we try to find them based on first impressions. When you have an amazing first meeting with someone or see a gorgeous Facebook photo, you idealize the person and automatically think they're going to be it. If a meeting doesn't go so well, you decide to overlook them. You have to get past the first impression and get down to the real person. Why do they want to be a part of your business? Do the two of you have a similar vision? Does this person have a real need for this business or the money? If you identify those reasons in the beginning, you have a better chance of finding someone who is a great fit.

Some partners might just be a fling, others you will date and break up with, and then there will be a few that you end up marrying. But there will be ups and downs to get to that place. You will encounter people of all shapes, sizes, colors, and backgrounds on this journey. You need all of these people—especially if you're in network marketing—because you want a beautiful, diverse circle of love. You won't have that if you select the same type of people all the time, so do your best to give everyone a fair shot.

DOS AND DON'TS

DOS

- **Reach out beyond family and friends.** Don't try to build your business by only asking and expecting your friends and family to buy from you.
- **Add value.** Show people you have something to give, that you are finding success, and that you know what you're doing.
- **Build your network one conversation at a time.** Be the best version of yourself and go out into the world to make others feel good. Say yes to every invitation. Attend networking events. Ask for referrals or meetings with people who are already successful. Hand out genuine compliments. Instead of being buried in your phone

while in line at Starbucks, use that time to make a new friend. You might be shocked at the number of people who have made amazing connections with strangers who are now customers and business partners. Put the phone down and be present in the moment. Turn strangers into friends, customers, referral sources, or partners.

- **Show interest.** One of the simplest things you can do to build your business is give someone an authentic compliment. Say, "Oh, my gosh. I love your shoes. Where did you get them?" Or "How old is your child? He's so cute." Whatever the compliment, it's an invitation to have a conversation. Also, never assume that someone stays at home and doesn't work just because they have a child. I ask everyone what they do for work. They'll tell me, and then nine times out of ten, they say, "What about you?" That's the perfect opportunity to make your elevator pitch. If you have another career besides your business, say, "Oh, I actually have two careers. I'm a nurse, and I also have an X business." You never know when somebody might be looking for exactly what you have to give!

DON'TS

- **Judge a person by what they are wearing or their social media profile.**
- **Leave the ball in their court.** Make the follow-up appointment. End the conversation strong.

- **Beg.** Teach and educate instead.
- **Take "no" as your final answer.** Follow up. Add value. And follow up until they are a yes!

PART III

Create Bonds (and Businesses) That Last Forever

Chapter Ten

BEYOND THE SECOND DATE

I remember my first day working as a real estate agent in Manhattan. I had just finished my weeklong training at the corporate headquarters. I walked into my office in the West Village, and my new manager showed me my desk, wished me luck, and left me there to sink or swim. I ate lunch by myself, and maybe one person talked to me. I basically had to figure out my new job all on my own.

I soon discovered that the New York City real estate industry was extremely transient. People came in and out through a revolving door, getting hired and fired, and the long-term agents weren't too keen on making friends with the newbies. Thankfully, I'm pretty personable and was eventually able to make friends.

I had a completely different experience when I started my network marketing business. People from all across the country with various levels of experience reached out to welcome me, to share their personal stories, and to cheer me on from the start. It was refreshing. I truly felt like people cared about me as a person and about my success. The onboarding experience was like nothing I had ever had before, and I realized it was paramount to building a culture that I wanted to be a part of. I couldn't wait to start building my own team!

As my business grew, I decided I wanted to create a positive experience for new people, too. I wanted them to feel like part of the team and included right away and not like they were alone on a desert island.

If you talk to anyone who works at a "Best Place to Work," they'll probably tell you they love their company because of the culture, the vision of the founders, and their coworkers. You want the same for your business! You want people to feel loved, appreciated, and that they are contributing to something important. When people feel like members of a community, they are much less likely to quit; they persevere because they feel that they are important, regardless of their level of success. You can't just focus on your top leaders and producers—everyone must feel important. Because each person *is* important. When everyone feels the love, it's a sure sign of a healthy culture and a thriving organization.

In network marketing, everyone has an equal opportunity to succeed. As a leader, you have to exhibit that this is true by treating everyone with respect. Any person who comes into your business could be the next superstar, and you want to treat them as such, until they prove that they aren't. It's an opposite concept than what we're used to: people actually have to disprove themselves. Love on everybody because people will surprise you!

A BETTER APPROACH

When you're starting a new relationship, what makes you feel good? You want to be introduced to your boyfriend's friends and made "official," you want to know that this person cares about you and will drop almost anything for you while you're in the honeymoon phase, and you want to feel safe and that you can share your true feelings—good and bad—with them.

It's the same when you bring on a new consultant to your team. You should introduce them to others to help them make friends and build relationships with accountability partners. At the end of the day, a job is not "just a job"—it's about feeling that you are part of something bigger than yourself (and having fun and feeling fulfilled while you do it). Friends, comrades, and peers who can strategize with you and offer support are one of the greatest pieces to creating meaning in your job.

If I didn't have the support of my peers early on in my business journey, I don't think I would have stuck with it. As women especially, we need people in our lives who are experiencing the same thing we are. For example, think back to planning your wedding: some people may have thought you were a bridezilla, but another bride probably understood how important the bridesmaids dresses and the menu font was going to be for you and was supportive.

In contrast, think back to when you were a clueless new mom. If you talked to the mother of teenagers, she probably rolled her eyes and said, "The newborn stage is easy. Wait until you have teenagers!" That mom did not offer any support because she had forgotten what it was like to have a newborn. Another new mom may have said or done something more helpful. It's the same with onboarding a new person and helping them build business relationships: you want to connect them with peers who are in a similar stage of the journey so they can help and support each other.

Sometimes I compare onboarding a new person to having a child. First, you potty train them. Then they're off to preschool and then to kindergarten. Once they're there, they go and make their own friends—you can't be their only friend or source of support. When new hires are social and make a lot of friends and peers, you set them up for success while continuing to work on your own business. I like to say, people join for the opportunity, but they stay for the community. You want to create an environment where people never want to leave.

GET PERSONAL

Within the first twenty-four to forty-eight hours of bringing on a new team member, set up a thirty-minute meeting to give them the opportunity to ask important questions (and for you to ask yours). What are their short- and long-term goals? How do they like to communicate? When will they make time to work their business? It's important for you to find out these details about them, but you also want to tell them what you expect. Court them and show them you will be a great mentor, leader, and friend.

You want to get to know your new partner as much as possible, so you'll talk on the phone a lot in the beginning. Make it clear in advance when the two of you will be talking and how often. And if you've set up a time to talk, they should know that you expect them to pick up the phone. End each call by setting the stage for the next one: "Great! I'll talk to you again on Wednesday at 8:00 p.m. If anything changes, let me know ahead of time." Let them know that the most successful consultants are the ones you speak with often, and they'll be excited and motivated to talk.

FLIRTING AND FEEDBACK

"Flirting" has an important role in onboarding. Text your new consultant daily, to just to say, "Hi, how are you today?" Make them feel excited and comfortable, and accentuate those wins. Show love to your new consultant and lead with a service mindset. Say things like, "I am so proud of you" and, "Great job!" Sometimes as leaders, we don't think of the skill that is required to build a big team—loving leadership must be at the front of your mind even if you've never been a leader before. Don't constantly talk about what a person has done wrong, needs to improve on, or might do wrong. Instead, highlight even the smallest victories; you're a cheerleader for your team.

People can be sensitive to negativity, especially in the beginning, because they might be unsure about doing something new. Even if you have to dig, find one good thing and talk about it. Focus on what they are doing right, if not exactly right, but even the fact that they are doing something that is moving them in the right direction. You can give constructive feedback or advice by giving them a compliment and then saying, "Here's something we can work on if you are interested." Choosing your words carefully can make a big difference.

You'll do a lot of hand-holding at first as you begin to court and flirt with new consultants, but then you'll start giving homework. Ask your team members to watch a certain video to prepare for your next meeting, or give them a small task or assignment that is due by a certain date. Their attitude and response to your requests will show you whether or not they really want to work and, as a by-product, whether or not you should continue to invest your precious time with them. Let them know you can guide and direct them as much as you can, but at the end of the day, you can't do the work for them. It's a partnership after all.

Setting these expectations and making these requests are important, but sadly, many people just won't do the work. If they start making excuses, you have to call them out. If you were dating them, you wouldn't put up with several canceled dates in a row, and you definitely can't tolerate it when building your business. Your time is valuable. You have to say something like, "You've said you want to build this, but your actions are telling me otherwise. What's going on with you? Is it something personal? Are you okay?" Don't be fearful. Put it out there, and do it right away. You can't waste time on someone who doesn't really want to be a part of your team, and they shouldn't waste time pretending.

RELATIONSHIPS CHANGE

When you start dating someone, the relationship usually follows a certain progression. You start with texting and talking every few days, then you move on to daily communication. Eventually, you share your deepest secrets, hopes, and dreams. After a while, if the relationship doesn't progress to saying those three special words, "I love you," and doing things like taking trips together and meeting each other's families, you absolutely need to have a conversation about where the relationship is going. If your partner's outlook on your relationship and where it's headed is different than yours, you shouldn't be giving them so much of your time.

The same goes for a professional relationship—you want to match people's efforts. You want to build a trusting and safe relationship with them if that's what they want, too.

For example, when I first started my business, I talked with my sponsor (the person who shared the business opportunity with me) almost every day for a year. We were both committed to growing our businesses, and we enjoyed working together. After the first year or so, we cut back on the phone calls and talked about once a week to strategize and catch up. Now, we talk about once or twice per month just to check in since we're both running large global teams, and she's more of a peer and friend rather than a mentor or teacher. I don't need her support as much as I used to, and that's a good thing! She knows I love her, and I know she loves me—the nature of our relationship has just evolved.

No matter the stage of your relationship with a team member, it's important to check in with people often to see how they're doing. This shows you care. Which, of course, you do, but sometimes people need to be reminded that you care and that you're thinking about them. If someone is sliding backward, you want to get in touch with them right away. If they aren't performing as well as they have in the past, you want to ask them about it. Ask if there's something going on in their personal life, or if there's anything you can help with. Find out their situation and avoid making assumptions. At the end of the day, people just want to know you care.

CALL IT OUT

It's okay to get comfortable in your relationships, but you never want to take anyone for granted. When my husband and I were dating in college, you couldn't send text messages or even call each other because we didn't have cell phones back then! *Crazy, right?* If Randy wanted to reach me, he had to call my dorm room, but he rarely called, which was frustrating, to say the least. I kept hoping to run into him on campus, and one day I woke up and realized this wasn't what I envisioned for our relationship. I mean, I thought I was a damn good catch! I was cute, fun, smart, and outgoing, and there were other guys who wanted to go out with me.

Randy was a few years older than me, and even though sometimes I felt like he was out of my league, something inside (it was probably my mother's voice) told me I needed a guy who would love and respect me. She used to say, "Find a man who treats you like a queen because you are!" I was usually strong and confident (thanks to my parents), and having this uneasy feeling all the time was not cool with me. I didn't like that this guy was making me chase him around. Although, isn't that how it always goes? We want the guy that doesn't seem to want us? Why do we torture ourselves?

That day, I decided I'd had enough, and when he stopped by my dorm room, I broke up with him. He was completely shocked! He didn't understand why I would end our romance, and I said, "If you want a girlfriend, you need to call her, take her out once in a while, and do what you say you're going to do." He begged me to stay with him, and I told him I'd consider it if he showed me that he really wanted to be with me. And you know what? He did!

So here is what I know: if I hadn't stood up for myself and told him he'd lose me if he didn't change, he probably would have continued to be nonchalant and assume that we were okay. I didn't want that to be the precedent in our relationship. And if he was distant and unreliable in the beginning, what would he be like later?

So often, people don't threaten to leave a relationship when they should. In business, if someone is not returning calls or meeting you halfway, you need to call them out. Say,

"Listen, you must not be into this like you told me you were. That's totally fine. I believe in you and think this is an amazing opportunity, but I can't spend my time with you if you're not going to give me yours." Your time is valuable. Don't forget that! When you call people out, it shows that you are confident—people understand that you're not messing around. If they want you as their mentor and partner, or if they want your help, they need to contribute to their half of the relationship.

It doesn't matter if you're dating, engaged, or working with someone professionally—show your confidence and worth, and command respect. If someone keeps standing you up, or they keep saying they're too busy, have a conversation. Ask if their goals have changed since the two of you last spoke, and tell them to let you know when they're ready to get back to work. Pair that with a homework assignment, and encourage them to resume their training.

EXPECT TO GET GHOSTED

About one in three people go into what we call in our industry the "Witness Protection Program." They join you, start their business, and then they ghost you. They get overwhelmed or nervous, or they talk to someone like a parent or friend who gives them a negative reaction about their new venture. They say they will meet with you later, and they don't, or they are unresponsive to texts and calls. If this happens, my advice is to check in two more times. Say, "Hey, hope everything's okay. Maybe you're busy or something has changed? I'm here for you when you need me. Just reach out when you're ready." This puts the responsibility back on them.

Don't chase people around, in business or in relationships. You don't want to be the girl who keeps texting the guy, "What are you doing this weekend?" And when he doesn't respond, she texts again, "Hey, I haven't heard from you. What's up?" Clearly, it's not working for him, or something is up, so have a conversation and end the relationship if necessary. You are way too strong and amazing to chase anyone around! Capisce?

Chapter Eleven

MORE "WE," LESS "ME"

I don't believe leadership is an inborn quality. It may come more naturally to some, but leadership skills can be learned. Many people have had leadership roles in their careers without even knowing it. Leadership is exhibited in many different ways, and the one thing that doesn't define it is a job title.

There's a girl on my team who has had some success in this business, but unfortunately, leadership does not come easy for her. She was great at building relationships and recruiting new people, but cultivating a great team culture and leading was not her strength. She says things like, "Why don't the people on my team want to work hard?" or, "I do everything right, but no one listens to me or cares."

I cringe at the posts on her team page—they're always about her and what she wants people to do. There's no talk about "our vision," or, "We can do this together," or, "I am so appreciative of this team." She's always at odds with someone, and she doesn't seem to understand why. As a leader, it's important to talk, lock arms with your team, treat them as equals, and never ever let them feel like you have an agenda. The more people you help succeed, the more it will benefit you organically over time.

One thing I know for sure through practice and experience is that leadership requires a lot of personal development—you have to work on yourself. As a leader, it's important to be a supporter and a coach, but you also need to gather feedback from others about how they view your leadership and how you can improve. What weaknesses do they see in you? What could use some work? Getting a promotion doesn't mean you automatically become a good listener—the skills don't magically appear with the title or role. Leadership is a verb and something you are constantly working on; you strive to keep getting better. It takes practice, and true leadership must be earned.

SUCCESS IS A SUCCESSFUL TEAM

What I love about network marketing is that people train others to do the same job they do. In corporate America, it's not uncommon to be trained or managed by someone who has never done your actual job. For me, my boss at my last corporate job was someone that I actually had to train. That still irks me! When that's the case, there's little opportunity for your boss to become your mentor. In network marketing, you learn and grow together, and you push one another to the next level. You can become more successful than the person who brought you into the business. It's a really fair business model.

Being in a leadership position doesn't give you the right to act like you're better than everyone else. Instead, it's about growing together—you can only be successful if your team is successful. Whether you are leading a team of two or two thousand in network marketing, or you're a business owner with employees, you receive compensation for other people's efforts.

In network marketing, your mindset as you lead and grow must always be one of, "I work for you, and I work with you," not, "I am your leader, and you must follow me." Leadership is often silent. Leadership is about service and love. When you lead with love and always look for ways to help others succeed, you will succeed, too. My goal has always been to make others feel that I am a member of the team. My success is theirs and vice versa. People need to know you're in the trenches right along with them; you aren't just talking the talk; you're walking the walk, too! The same is true in other industries also: leadership isn't about the title;

it's about the way you make people feel. The best and most respected leaders are humble and don't forget where they came from. They don't change or act above others as their success grows.

When a team has a winning record in sports, people often say it's because they had a great coach, they had strong leadership, and there was a sense of camaraderie. Culture is key. Even in sports, everyone on the team needs to feel like they made an important contribution. Good leaders constantly thank team members for doing their part, highlight the good, reflect on the not so good, and push them out of their comfort zone. They encourage growth and they expect more.

People work harder when they feel appreciated, so leaders can't make the mistake of only highlighting their top performers over and over again. Don't just focus on the A team; show the B team some love, too! Help develop your B players into A players, and your business will soar! You can't build your business by relying on two or three superstars. There's more success when everyone excels at every level.

Creating in-person bonds and relationships is very important to build trust and a happy, cohesive organization. It is important to come together from time to time, whether in a small group setting or a larger group retreat. Think about ways you can spend time with your top leaders, as well as your part-time side-hustlers. When I was first building this business, I announced a team retreat on a beach in Florida. I honestly didn't know who might qualify for it, but I knew that *I* would run very hard for a trip like this and for recognition, and so maybe others would, too. That retreat changed my life, and I met incredible women on my team who became top leaders and remain my friends to this day.

ADOPT THE "WE" MENTALITY

When you address your team, be mindful of the phrases you use. Say things like, "I think we should be doing more of this. What do you think?" rather than, "This is what I want you to do." That little change in verbiage makes a huge difference! Even if you just start replacing "I" with "we," it can have a positive impact. Every time you are training, coaching, or meeting with your team, make sure to emphasize that you wouldn't be where you are without them. By making this acknowledgment, you create a positive vibe and team vision.

Here's a tip: if you end up getting a promotion or special recognition for an accomplishment, openly thank and highlight everyone else and their contributions to your success. Celebrate your people!

BEING IMPERFECT IS PERFECT

Let's jump back to the team leader who was stuck in the "I" mentality. People talked with her about trying a different approach, but she wasn't interested in changing. She said there was nothing wrong with her communication style. She simply felt her team didn't appreciate her. I stepped up and checked in on some of her team members who asked me for help, while she continued to reject the feedback she received. Every new drama, dispute, or conversation led to a negative outcome.

To be perfectly honest, in my many years of network marketing, I can count the number of altercations I've had with others on one hand. I'm no expert, and I make it clear that I'm not perfect while still putting my best foot forward. I'll say things like, "I could be wrong, but this new approach could work." I try to share what I think will genuinely help others, and I'm willing to admit when I'm unsure or when I'm wrong. When I am wrong in any way, I am very quick to apologize. I want the team to know that we're all human together. Humility is the greatest quality you can have as a leader.

Great leaders don't tell people what they're doing wrong. They ask them! Don't go on and on about what they need to change. Ask them what they believe their strengths and weaknesses are. This approach is highly effective because people inherently know where they excel and where they struggle. Instead of telling them what you think, let them give you the answer. You can take your coaching to the next level by allowing your people to be their own problem solvers.

It's easy to expect people to change overnight. Let's say you're dating a guy and you have plans for the weekend. You're hanging out with him, and his friends walk up and ask him what he's doing on Saturday. You'd fully expected him to say, "My girlfriend and I are hitting the beach," right? But instead, he says, "I'm going to the beach on Saturday." Wouldn't you find that odd? You'd probably think, "I know because I'm going to the beach, too—with you, asshole!"

When you're dating someone, you want to face the world together and always feel like you are important and you matter to your partner. But people make mistakes, and how you handle or admit your mistakes dictates the future of a relationship. The same goes for you and your business team. It takes time and effort to build and grow strong relationships of respect and trust. It takes months, if not years, to create a strong camaraderie, but it can take even longer to fix mistakes and mend hurt feelings, so it's best to start (and maintain) a healthy team mentality and culture. You're all in this together!

Chapter Twelve

PUBLIC DISPLAYS OF AFFECTION IN BUSINESS

Consider a kid whose mom never comes to his athletic events. Maybe she works crazy hours, or maybe there's another reason she can't fit them into her schedule. What if, one day, she shows up to his baseball game? The kid is shocked, right? After he picks his jaw up off the ground, he grins from ear to ear, he's on his A game, and he plays his heart out. He does his best because his mom is there, watching and supporting him.

Recognizing people and showing them appreciation is the right thing to do, but it also has benefits. They won't just feel the love—they will be ultra-motivated when they know that you are watching. Your attention and support will motivate others, build the culture, and your work relationships will improve, too.

I'm not perfect, but I do my best to let my team members know that I always have their backs and am willing to work hard with them. That goes for everyone, whether they're a top or minimal producer. I let them know I'm willing to get my hands dirty. I'm not just sitting on a hilltop and shouting out orders like a queen.

I once heard about a CEO who regularly had lunch with mail-room employees and spent time with people who worked on every floor of his building. Some of the employees didn't even know he was the CEO because he was social, cool, and approachable. He asked them questions and wanted to know the good and the bad about the company he was running. He didn't judge people or make anyone feel like they weren't good enough. I believe wholeheartedly in this approach.

You have to be approachable and socialize with your people. If you see a team member in public, say hello and ask, "How are you?" Give them a genuine hug. You should treat the people who work in your organization like family, because without them, you might not be able to feed your own family. *Capisce?* Talk to them. Listen to them instead of acting like you don't have time for conversation. I can't stand it when managers, senior execs, or top leaders act like they're too good to associate with the people who work for them. Don't let this be you! So much of a person's fulfillment in any relationship comes from feeling recognized and appreciated. Throughout the years, I've had friends who've complained that their boyfriends were very attentive in private but ignored them in public. This definitely happened to me in my college days, and it stung! You can't behave that way in business. PDA, short for Public Displays of Affection, at work is a good thing!

You show affection to your people by recognizing them for activity and productivity. Public recognition is a key component to building your business, creating a positive culture, and having happy consultants and employees. Ask yourself these questions: Do you recognize your people publicly and privately on a regular basis? Do you openly and affectionately tell team members and people in your organization that you're proud of them? Do you make their accomplishments known? If not, now is definitely the time to start!

PDA: A HOW-TO GUIDE

To begin showing PDA to your team, I suggest creating a Facebook page or website where you can post newsletters, team emails, photos, and announcements. You can also use the page to recognize people for huge promotions and small accomplishments—there are no rules. Just keep it positive and spread the love! Recognize new consultants and team members, congratulate your top 10, 100, or 250 (depending on team size) salespeople of the month, and acknowledge promotions. Give a shout-out to the people who are just plain killing it, or those who are doing the right things but maybe don't have the results yet.

Create a system so you rotate through different types of recognition, giving everyone a chance to see their name on the page from time to time. Public recognition among peers is the ultimate motivator, and people will work for it.

THE SELF-SHOUT-OUT

An even simpler and effective way to recognize and build buzz in your organization is to have people recognize themselves! You can ask people to comment on a post once they complete a task or hit a certain milestone, and people love it! On a team meeting or an in-person event, invite people to announce out loud a recent accomplishment, big or small. I don't want to say humans love to brag, but we do love to tell our peers when we've accomplished something. This self-shout-out creates momentum and excitement. Why? When team members see that others have completed a task and been recognized, they want to complete one for themselves, too! It also makes the accomplished team members feel good since they can publicly acknowledge what they've done without bragging.

CHANGE IT UP

It's important to highlight different people for different reasons so everyone gets a boost. Sometimes, I recognize top performers, and other times, I recognize people for giving the most effort or simply just doing an activity or showing up. Sometimes, I make a big deal about someone who is new and starting to make waves, and other times, I give a shout-out to someone who has been consistently performing well for a long time or winning a contest. When I change up the types of recognition, it makes it difficult for team members to compare themselves to one another, and they realize they can all shine in different lights.

GROUP HUG

If you're facilitating a training or you're at a team or company event, make sure to thank everyone who helped you. Thank volunteers while you are addressing the group, and recognize the people who made a contribution to the event. Publicly praise team members who received promotions. Show that you are a supportive leader, you are excited when your people do well, and that you are thankful for everyone. When you praise others for doing things they aren't being compensated for, it makes others want to help, too.

BEHIND CLOSED DOORS

I understand some people don't like PDA. Generally, these

people don't like their partners to hold hands with them or kiss them in public. However, when it comes to showing affection in private, it's a completely different story.

When you give recognition behind closed doors, it's usually a pleasant surprise. When someone does something incredible, they know that they've earned a big shout-out. When you personally acknowledge something that may seem small, though, it can mean even more to them.

Say something like, "Hey, I see you. You're working hard, you're doing what you're supposed to be doing, and I'm excited to see what you'll accomplish in the future." This approach is especially helpful and appropriate when someone overcomes a private struggle or isn't getting the results they want for some time even though they are doing the work. It shows you've noticed their effort over their victory, but you know not to embarrass them by making a public announcement. Encouraging them privately protects their feelings and ensures that you don't betray that person's trust.

Private recognition is also appropriate when only a handful of people have achieved a certain milestone, and there may be some sensitivity attached to others who were running for it but missed. For example, let's say some of your team members were running for a promotion or an incentive, and a couple of them didn't get it. Your basic, emotional intelligence tells you that a public shout-out right away may not be the best way to congratulate those who achieved this milestone. In this case, a phone call, a handwritten note, or a gift of flowers would be much better. Or if you do publicly recognize the ones who deserve it, you might want to reach out to the ones who missed and give them a little confidence boost. You aren't "dating" just one person in your business and on your team. You have a lot of people to love on, so be sure to do it carefully.

JUST BECAUSE

I used to hate flowers. When I was a kid, flowers on the table meant my parents just had a fight, and my dad was attempting to make up with my mom. Instead of being beautiful reminders of spring time, Caribbean vacations, or weddings, they were filed in my head under the letter F— they reminded me of funerals and fights. Flowers weren't in the house often, but when I saw them, I knew it was my father's way of saying, "Sorry."

After some training and grooming, my dad began to realize that he should give flowers to my mother randomly. He started to bring flowers home after work, or he'd pick them up from the grocery store for no special reason at all. Good job, Dad!

Early on, I told my husband that I didn't want flowers after a fight. I only wanted them when he felt like giving them to me, a "just because I love you" gift. Believe it or not, all of this relates to your business! You don't have to wait for someone to get promoted to send notes, flowers, or otherwise make a special gesture. Anytime is the right time to let others know that you care about them. When giving gifts to your team members, you should do it randomly just because. There doesn't always need to be a special reason for it. Yes, you can absolutely give gifts for birthdays or holidays, but throw in those special gifts or acknowledgments, too! This has been easy for me because I enjoy gift giving, but if it doesn't come naturally to you, you may have to make an effort here.

You can send a gift to someone who had a rough day and needs a pick-me-up, or you can send it simply because you're proud of the work they're doing. You can include a note that says, "I'm so proud of you! Keep it up!"

DON'T PUT IT OFF

Sometimes, we wait to take action. We've all done it at one time or another. A friend has a birthday coming up, and we think we'll call her later. Then you go about your day, you forget about it, and you realize it the next morning and feel like such a jerk! So what should you have done? You have to stop putting things off. The moment the thought enters your mind to do something kind or make someone feel good, make that call, or you will forget. Stop what you're doing and take care of it right then and there.

When a team member accomplishes something great, I try to acknowledge it right away. I also reach out immediately when I have a concern. I'll say something like, "Hey, I haven't heard from you in a while. Is everything all right?" Both situations require timely responses so I can be as helpful as possible, as quickly as possible.

People are people, and you have to support them through the good and the bad. When you recognize them for the good, it motivates them to work harder. When you're there for the bad, it counts. If you see someone struggling, don't wait until a convenient time to contact them. You don't want to see this person a week later and say, "I've been meaning to call." How will they know you're being truthful? All they know is that you didn't, and they might even be hurt or a little angry. To be your best self, you can't procrastinate when it comes to meaningful human contact, especially when someone might need your help.

GIFTING AS A LOVE LANGUAGE

As a leader, you communicate appreciation for your people by thanking them and openly giving recognition, but gift giving is another effective way to let them know that. When you're doing well, and the team is doing well, it's easy to feel compelled to give gifts. It's something that actually makes me feel good inside, too!

You can use gifts to create fun team contests and raffles, or you can have a spotlight or showcase a gift as an incentive and give it as a prize to the top achiever of the month. Remember, gifts don't always have to be tangible things. Experiences make amazing gifts, too. Some gifts that have been a hit with my team are group happy hours, dinners, special get-togethers with me, or a donation to a favorite charity.

Incentives are also important in any sales organization. When creating a strategy to implement incentives into your business, think about the people on your team who need to be motivated the most. Who are they? Your top-, middle-, or bottom-tier people? Is there a way that you can motivate all of them? Are you able to provide different and appropriate incentives? Here's a tip: motivating a lot of people to do just a little bit more will yield better results than hugely motivating one outlier.

If you're at a loss for ideas for incentives, it's okay to ask people what motivates them. Ask, "What motivates you? Are you internally or externally motivated? Do you want gifts, recognition, or special time with me or with others?" You can figure this out with your team and then pair the appropriate milestone with the incentive. When I first started, I was motivated by extra income. I needed to pay my bills, but I also hated cleaning my apartment. Making enough extra money to hire a cleaning person would have been beyond awesome. Others might have been motivated by a luxury purse, but I just wanted to pay someone to scrub my toilet!

You might find that some people on your team are not motivated by money. They might value giving to charity, quality time with friends and family, or a date night with their spouse. Some people just really enjoy going out to dinner, so a restaurant gift certificate might be a huge incentive for them. You never know! Just keep in mind that everyone is different and that you have to assess individual and team goals when choosing incentives. You also have to give yourself a budget for this, too. A certain percentage of your business income each month works well. Figure out what is going to elicit the best response, and then go for it.

WHAT DO YOU WANT FROM ME?

If you don't want to ask every team member on an individual basis, "Hey, what motivates you?" you can always create a survey. You can offer it to just your top team members, or you can offer it to everyone. Either way, majority rules when it comes to you making your decision. Don't make the mistake of choosing only the answers you agree with, and don't default to using incentives that may have worked for you or others in the past. This is about motivating your current team. Oh, and make sure the survey is anonymous!

The best incentives are the ones that get people to work a little harder—to get them to stretch for a goal. They also should encourage people to go above and beyond; incentives need to be exciting and encourage people to do more than just a little above the minimum. You'll discover that incentives will show you who is truly driven and who you should be trying to develop. The superstars may change from year to year, but offering an incentive for people who can beat their numbers from the previous year will show you who is hungry and willing to rise to the challenge right now.

You can also motivate your people (and positively impact your bottom line) by offering a relatively free incentive. This could be a personalized training call with you or inviting them to your home for coffee or a cocktail. These types of incentives are easy to offer on a monthly or quarterly basis, and you can use them to move your team forward. What if everyone happens to hit the goal? I guess you'll be making a lot of drinks that month and will have to be resourceful to stay within your means!

INVITATIONS: ASK FOR WHAT YOU WANT

From time to time, other leaders will come to me with complaints that no one on their team steps up to collaborate or help. I always ask them what the invitation looked like. The reply will be something like, "Well, I posted on our team page that I needed volunteers, and nobody was willing to help."

No wonder nobody came forward—impersonal posts don't get a lot of play. A blast email or post asking for something rarely gets responses, or you'll keep getting the same people over and over. If you want fresh people, you need to get out there and ask them! People want to be invited—they want to be selected to help. If you want volunteers or need help with a project, you have to call or write people individually. Let them know why you're reaching out to them and why you think they'd be a great fit for what you're doing. Tell them you appreciate them, and let them know how participation benefits them.

TRACK WHAT WORKS

You absolutely need to track incentives and their results as part of your system. Analyze your numbers and record what has worked well. Keep track so you know that X incentive took you from point A to point B. If you have an impeccable system of tracking, you'll find that usually what worked once will work again.

Be prepared to make some mistakes with incentives—I

know I have. I've spent money only to find I didn't get a lot of movement or reward from it, but I learned from each experience. I believe I've been able to move forward in business because I learn from my mistakes and try not to repeat them. The bottom line? Have fun and experiment with incentives and giving. If you keep coming up with new ideas, you and your team could be pleasantly surprised by the results!

HAPPINESS ABOVE ALL

The happiness of your team members is much more important than their success. People often think they'll be happy once they make a certain amount of money or achieve a certain goal. That may be true, but you want your people to be happy while they are working toward their goal. Much of the happiness will come from sharing the victory with others, and knowing they were appreciated along the way.

Some of the most successful people are the loneliest, so you want to make sure that your top producers always have your full support, even if they don't ask for it. Celebrate them during the entire journey. Milestones come and go, but the camaraderie and joy you both can get from the process is the best part. I promise.

Chapter Thirteen

LOVE CONQUERS ALL

I was at a company event when a consultant came up to me and said, "I wish I was on your team because my sponsor who brought me into the business doesn't appreciate me. She has her favorites, and I'm not one of them, and sometimes it makes me want to quit and rejoin another team." Her words made me sad because it was obvious that this woman wanted to be included as a leader and appreciated, but her sponsor wasn't helping her achieve this goal.

Unfortunately, I hear these stories all the time. Every time I hear them, they serve as a reminder that emotional care is important, especially with women. No one wants to feel like they are less than others, especially when they're doing well. It's imperative that you let all producers know how valuable they are to you and the team. And sometimes this means having tough-love conversations, too.

Unfortunately, I saw conflict and tears behind the scenes early on. Team members may not always tell their leaders or sponsors how they feel, but they will tell one another. It's possible that people on my team have said negative things about me behind my back, and if they did, I sincerely hope they know I would never mean to hurt anyone! However, at the end of the day, it's important to give people grace.

If someone tells their sponsor they're feeling devalued and nothing changes, then that can lead to huge problems. The team member begins to feel like the ignored middle child of the business family, and you don't want anyone to feel like that. It's only human to like certain people better than others, but you can't give preferential treatment, and you definitely can't blow someone off who wants to develop themselves professionally and grow their business—especially if you're the one who brought them on.

Don't play favorites. Try to love on everyone equally; favoritism ruins camaraderie and creates a toxic culture. It destroys relationships, hurts people's feelings, and causes the slighted people to underperform. There are absolutely no benefits to playing favorites.

You want people to make the most of the business opportunity that is before them. You don't want them to stop trying because they think that nobody notices them or nobody cares. There are all types of personalities in families, and since the people in your business are considered family, you need to accept them all.

HEART-CENTERED LEADERSHIP

If you show love all the time, you'll become known as a loving leader. Your reputation will precede you, and you'll build a strong, loving team culture because people know you care. Never begin a conversation with business, unless you have a real business emergency. Don't start out with, "Hey! So where are you this month? Are you going to hit your goal?" You always want to lead with a few minutes of, "How are you? How was your weekend? What are the kids up to? What's new?" Be real and be humble. Be normal and be cool. Be a human being first.

Think about it. How would you feel if every time your husband called you, he started the conversation with, "Did you do the dishes? What are you making for dinner?" You'd rather he starts by asking you about your day and then telling you about his. "Hi, honey, how was your day? Oh, great. No, we didn't land that account, but that's okay. By the way, what are you thinking for dinner? Can I help you in the kitchen?"

As a leader, you have to get to know people beyond their numbers—get to know them personally. Learn about their family life, their past, and their future goals. This not only builds strong working relationships; it also helps you figure out how to better serve them. After all, leadership is service!

In a great organization, people feel loved and noticed. When I coach other leaders, I ask them to tell me the last time they openly recognized a team member and the last time they called someone to say they appreciated them. I try to find out when they last thanked someone for doing an outstanding job. I'll get replies like, "Oh, I've never done that," or, "I did it once last year." Once the leader realizes they haven't been showing their people much appreciation, they quickly change their ways.

I talk about getting to know your team members, but I didn't always do a good job with this. I made my share of mistakes. I once had a new team member who was doing an awesome job, and we talked business every time we met or talked on the phone. I thought everything was going well and that we were building a strong business relationship *and* friendship. Later, I found out that she was getting separated and had been dating a new man for six months—I couldn't believe I didn't know that! I thought we were close, but I realized I didn't get to know her well enough personally. She always asked me about my family, but our business conversations were so strong that I guess I never asked about hers. I was not being a good leader, and ever since then, I make it a point to get to know my team members personally and be aware of what is happening in their lives.

In this rushed digital age, we text, email, and send messages over apps and social media instead of picking up the phone to talk, and in doing so, our intent can get lost in translation. Whether online or in person, start your conversations with personal questions—this one change can make a world of difference. And another tip, adding smiley faces, hearts, and friendly emojis always makes a text or email seem friendlier.

ACTIONS SPEAK LOUDER THAN WORDS

We've all had a friend who had a boyfriend who didn't really act like he wanted to be with her. Sure, he said he did, but he never showed it—he put zero effort into the relationship and just expected her to stick around. Eventually, your friend made the right decision and let him go.

As a leader, I've had to call people out when they acted like this boyfriend—their actions didn't match their words. If someone tells me they want to advance in title, but then all they do is complain, there's a major inconsistency between their actions and their words. If I'm spending time coaching them, but they aren't putting in the necessary work, I'm going to speak up like a disgruntled girlfriend, right? I'll say, "You tell me you want to be with me, but we never see each other. You don't act like you want to be with me, and you aren't pulling your weight. I'm not happy in this relationship."

Just like your man (or woman) needs to show you they love you, your team members have to show you, not just tell you, they want to meet their goals and will do whatever it takes to get there. Otherwise, you can't spend all your valuable time helping them. If that sounds harsh, it's because it is! The key to approaching this conversation gently and correctly is by focusing on the relationship.

LOVE AND EXPECTATIONS

In any growing sales organization, you will find the top achievers—they're the go-getters who always have their eye on the prize. They hit the ground running, never stop, and they usually don't just hit their goal, they slide right past it. On the flip side, a business also usually has average or lower producers—the people who always seem to hit the minimum or just a dollar above. You have to be kind and show love to both categories of people, and in doing so, you just might spur on a low producer to become a top performer. With a little effort and action on their part, they can change their outcomes.

If someone tells you they want a promotion or to really take their business to the next level and they mess up a few times, or they do something that is inconsistent with their words, give them another chance. Maybe they apologize and say, "I'm so sorry. I was just so busy and couldn't get to it." These things happen, and it's okay. Kids get sick, people go through bouts of depression, or they have to put out fires at their full-time job. You always want to give people grace. However, if it becomes a habit, or they keep coming up with excuses, that's a clear indicator that this person doesn't really want to move up in the ranks. You can continue to support them, but don't be so giving of your time.

Ironically, you will find that your lowest producers are some of the biggest complainers, and you'll need to exercise tough love with them. Before they have a chance to complain again about their poor results, give them a task to complete before your next meeting or call. Say, "Let's talk next week at the same time. But before we do, I want you to read this chapter in (X) book and then make a list of all of your current prospects. Do you think you can do that?" If they say yes, then you follow up by saying, "Great, but if you don't get done with your homework in time, then let me know, and we can reschedule for when you do get to finish it!" Sadly, 80 percent of people are not going to call. They'll apologize and tell you they didn't have the time to finish the assignment, and you can breathe easy knowing you did what you could to help them. They just aren't ready to advance or give the business the time it needs, and it's not your fault. I will repeat: it's NOT your fault.

Let's go back and imagine that you didn't give that assignment. The team member would have called with the same issues and complaints, and you'd have the same conversation. Nothing would have changed, and you both would have wasted precious time. And time equals money. You could have spent that time working with someone who was truly motivated or working on your own sales. Tasks and deadlines push people to action, place a clear value on your time, and reveal who is willing to put in the work.

WORK WITH THE WILLING

Schools, hospitals, restaurants, spas, and ecommerce businesses all have issues, and your business will have them, too. Your mindset and the way in which you navigate your business's issues will determine your success. You will work with complainers who view the glass as half empty, and you'll work with amazing, positive people, who view the glass as half full.

Someone once told me, "Work with the willing and *love* the rest." If they're willing to do the work, take action and put forth effort, then invest your time in them. Tell the others, "I care for you, and I appreciate you. You're doing great, but I can't spend a lot of time coaching you if you're not putting in the work. It's not fair to me or to the people who are showing real effort and commitment." These words tell the person that you'll still love on them; you just won't invest your time developing them for growth that they clearly don't want.

FAMILY AND FRIENDS DON'T GET BENEFITS

There is no one I love and respect more than my amazing mother. We love hard, and I fight with her more often than anyone else in the world. I honestly tell her how I feel, and she gives it to me straight, too—she definitely tells me more than a friend or stranger ever would! Now, picture the two of us working together.

You have to walk a fine line and find balance if you work with close friends and family. You have to set boundaries and expectations from the beginning. Say, "This is a business relationship. I'm going to treat you just like everyone else—I won't single you out, but I also won't show favoritism toward you. I will work alongside you and match your efforts and be your biggest cheerleader. What you produce won't make me love you any more or any less." Have that conversation up front, keep the lines of communication open, and tell your friend or family member that they need to call you out if you do something that bothers them—make it a two-way street.

Once you and your loved one are in agreement, treat your working relationship like it's brand new. It's separate from your personal lives. From there, do your best to keep them separate. When you're together, continue with your boundaries. Say, "Okay, we're going to talk business for the next ten minutes, and then we'll chat about real life."

Of course, all of that is easier said than done, but you don't want to create awkward situations. You don't want your friend to not pick up the phone when you call because she thinks you want to talk business or thinks you want her to produce more—maybe you just want to talk!

TOUGH LOVE

Everyone wants to know that someone is in their corner and rooting them on, but there will come a time when you'll need to correct someone or even give criticism. In fact, it's inevitable that you'll have issues with some people. If someone doesn't play by the rules or repeatedly makes mistakes, you have to address these problems.

To handle these tough conversations the right way, I considered a lesson I learned in my marriage. One day, my husband told me I didn't praise or thank him enough for the work he was doing around the house. That stung. He said, "You never praise me for the things I do—you just scold me for what I didn't do. I do the dishes all the time, and you don't thank me. You're just mad that I didn't clean the counter the way you wanted." *Ouch!* So I made it a point to thank him more often for doing the dishes. And guess what? After I started doing that, he cleaned the counter more often, too! Through this experience, I learned that people want to be praised for even the most minimal accomplishments because it motivates them to work harder. This is a helpful hint to strengthen relationships in your business, marriage, family, and with friends!

I also learned to always begin a criticism with positive feedback or praise. When it's time to have a tough conversation with a team member, always start with praise. My mother-in-law shared that tip with me a while ago, and it really is helpful! I start by saying something like, "I think you're doing a great job with X, Y, and Z, and everyone loves X about you. But I see you struggling in this certain area, and I'd love to offer you some guidance, if you'd like." That approach is kind and gentle, and you'll get a better response than if you had said, "You are doing it all wrong. You obviously need me to help you." When you model loving leadership, your team will duplicate it with one another. It's difficult to navigate the waters of people's expectations and emotions, but with careful planning and common sense, it's possible to do it well.

To build your business and encourage your team members, you must set a standard. If you continue to waste time without strong systems in place, shame on you. That's not good leadership. Essentially, that's taking money out of your pocket. You're wasting time on people who have no agenda or plan. You have to have an action plan in place so time is not wasted.

Don't be harsh with people, but show them tough love. It's

the same kind of love you would give to your spouse if they didn't keep a promise. Say, "I'm not going to remind you to clean out the garage again, but I'm not going to cook your dinner this week until it's done. Sorry."

With tough love, remember, the emphasis is on the love. If you want your team to take you seriously, you have to put this system in place. Your success demands it!

Chapter Fourteen

FROM LOVE TO LEADERSHIP

A few years ago, my husband, an avid cyclist, was in a near tragic accident. It was right after we'd had our second child, and he was just heading back to work after enjoying two months of paternity leave. He rode in a commuter club with other cyclists over the George Washington Bridge from New Jersey into Manhattan. The day of the accident, the guy who usually rode in front was on vacation, and my husband was in the front and got hit by a car that accidently turned when it shouldn't have.

That morning, I got a phone call from a social worker at the hospital, telling me I needed to get there right away. I arrived to find my husband on a stretcher, surrounded by ten people in the room, including the police. He came out of the accident with a broken neck, shoulder, arm, ribs, and lots of cuts and bruises. But he was alive and could walk; his helmet saved his life that day.

MANAGING THE ROAD TO RECOVERY

At the time of the accident, I had already built a substantial network marketing business, made incredible friends, and helped to shape other amazing leaders. Since we had such a great camaraderie, my team leaders stepped in and said, "We want you to take time off. You need to be home with your husband and take care of him. We'll manage the team for you."

My husband and I still talk about this all the time. People came up to us and said, "I can't believe what bad luck you've had. You just had a baby, and now Randy is at home injured."

But we would say, "We can't believe how lucky we are. Randy is okay, we don't have to hire a nurse, we can afford to pay these extra medical bills, and nobody has to return to work full time."

I was able to fully focus on helping Randy with his recovery and not worry about my team or my business going anywhere because we had established great systems and developed great leaders over the years. I still get choked up thinking about that time and the incredible people on our team who stepped in to cover for me. This is one of the extraordinary things about network marketing.

PRODUCERS VS. LEADERS

First and foremost, not everyone is meant for leadership. I am a big believer that leadership truly isn't a title but an action. Some people just don't want to be a leader and just want to work and only focus on themselves. That is totally fine! The default thinking is that top producers are the ones who should rise into leadership, but often times, your top sales producers are happy where they are—they want to continue selling and hitting their own personal sales goals. Just because someone can sell, that doesn't mean they possess leadership qualities. They could be more of a worker and truly want nothing to do with managing and helping others grow.

If you try to force a top seller into leadership, it can backfire. Pushing a sales superstar might be a mistake, and I saw this happen often in real estate. Top performers were promoted to vice president, and they were suddenly in charge of leading a team. It wasn't long before the business fell apart because the person didn't know how to delegate or share responsibility—they preferred to sell and do everything on their own. The leader and the team crashed and burned because the leader didn't belong there in the first place.

How, then, do you make the distinction between leaders and producers? You have to observe their behaviors and personality traits. Leaders are givers and want to help others. They show a drive to develop people, teach, and give their time to help others succeed. Producers or salespeople want to grow their own numbers, beat their own goals, and focus on their personal customers. Which is wonderful! Leaders think about the future and create a vision; producers usually think metrics for the present month and enjoy the day-to-day hustle. Leaders step into the foreground when needed and also know when to hide in the background and let others rise up; producers often want rewards and recognition. Leaders get fulfillment seeing others who they've helped thrive.

LEADERS VS. SALESPEOPLE

LEADERS	SALESPEOPLE
Give their time to others.	Focus on their own sales.
Think about the long-term vision.	Focus on the short-term goal.
Learn and teach others.	Learn.
Make quick decisions that will benefit the group.	Ask for advice.
Push people to the front to shine.	Want to be highlighted and acknowledged.

When choosing a new person to develop, pick someone who knows how to work with others, delegate, cope with drama, and enjoys helping others succeed. Teach humility, service, and gratitude in addition to the ins and outs of the business. Someone once told me that the best leaders are the ones who have coached and trained so many leaders that if they go away for a week, the operation thrives and continues to run smoothly, even when they aren't on-site or present for some time.

If you think someone might be a good leader, find out what they want first. Ask, "Do you want to be a salesperson, or do you want to lead? Do you want to lead a team of salespeople? I'm asking you because I see potential in you." Many people don't understand what leadership entails, so it's best to set expectations with them up front.

LET IT GO: A LESSON IN DELEGATION

When I was transitioning from real estate sales into management, I had a meeting with the head of my company a few months after I started my managerial position. He'd just returned from a leadership retreat about delegation, and he wanted to share what he had learned. He said that the best leaders are the ones who trained others well enough that when they delegate a task, they truly let it go and don't micromanage.

He said that delegation is a process. You hand a task over, assess how the person did, and then coach them on how to improve—talk with them about what they did well and what they can do better next time. Then you hope they do it right the next time. You do all of this, but you absolutely do not micromanage. That is the worst thing a leader can do.

When you micromanage people, you are saying, "I know I asked you to do this, but I don't really trust you will do it right." If you give someone an assignment, it's no longer yours. Let it go. It may not be easy to do at first, but you need to do it so your people can grow, and so you can earn the trust and respect of your team. Let people fail a little so they can learn. Praise what they did well, and if you truly think something needs to be changed, tell them how you think they can improve it.

My former boss didn't just coach in delegation, he demonstrated it. He trained me well, and whenever he left, he said, "Miriam, you're in charge. If you need me, you know how to reach me, but I trust you." I ran the office pretty often, and I grew as a person and an employee because he had mastered the art of delegation.

As a leader who is building a business, it's your job to cultivate as many leaders as possible. If you are comfortable taking a week off because you know all will be well without you and that business will still grow, that's a clear sign of a healthy organization. People may think a leader needs to have their nose in every detail and be present for everything, but that's not true. They also need to be able to step back and let their people and systems take over. The ultimate goal of leadership is to enable others to rise to the top with you. It is lonely at the top if you are all by yourself!

TO DEVELOP PEOPLE INTO LEADERS

If someone has the goal of being a team leader, you can begin helping them with personal development. This will get the ball rolling but will also help to determine if it's truly what they want. Give them opportunities to learn and step up, and if they follow through, that will show you that they are in it to win it—they will rise for a challenge. Test the waters by asking them to join you at an event. Say, "I'm doing a presentation, and I'd like for you to come up for a couple of minutes and share your story with the group." Ask them to send you their notes and a practice video first, and give them feedback. After the event, assess how they did. Were they prepared? Did they do well? You can also ask them to join you on a training call to share some tips. How did they perform? Talk with the person afterward, and give positive feedback before any constructive criticism. This sets them up for success, and they'll learn to duplicate this practice with their people in the future.

Some people will crumble when they get their feet wet with cultivating leadership, and they may not want to try it again. That's perfectly fine, but you shouldn't give up on them yet; analyze what happened, and encourage them to give it another shot later. However, once a true leader gets a taste of how rewarding it is to help others succeed, they will want more. They'll want to get back onstage again, and they'll want to start developing people. These are the people you want to invest your time in. Help them win and you will win, too!

PREPARE YOUR PEOPLE

Make sure to prepare and equip your leaders for success. You can't just throw them into an event without any preparation or give them new tasks without properly training them first. If you do, they may fail miserably and never want to do it again. And who could blame them? If this happens, it's not their failure. It's yours. As a leader, you failed to prepare them.

If you hang people out to dry, they will resent you. If you've pushed them too hard, they might even give up on the idea of stepping into leadership roles. Give them a little bit at a time, and let them ask for more when they're ready.

My son plays soccer, and one of his coaches told the parents, "You can't just sit there and yell at the kids to work harder. Give constructive criticism after the game by telling your child what to work on next time. Yelling doesn't work." Similarly, you don't want to be the boss that constantly tears people down with no analysis.

Check in with people as you build up new leaders. Ask peers for their impression of your leaders in training. Getting an outside perspective can help because sometimes our own is skewed if we're too close to the situation. We may have warm feelings toward someone because personally they're great, but maybe the public doesn't agree. Everyone has a favorite, so you want those checks and balances in place. You're not perfect, so get an objective view to see the whole picture.

A TEAM APPROACH

Lastly, treat developing leaders as equals. When talking with them, use words like "we" and "us." Share your plans with them before you announce them to the rest of the field. Show respect for them by gathering their input before you move forward with decisions. Don't go above their heads and launch something new without sharing with them first and asking for feedback. In order for something to work and move the needle, you need buy-in, especially from your leaders.

Ultimately, it's your business, and you have the final say, but you might miss out on new perspectives and great advice if you bypass your up-and-coming leaders. Asking for their input not only helps you; it sets them up to be part of the success. When you announce a new project or initiative, you can give them credit for their contribution!

I've worked with some so-called leaders in the past who asked me for input and then took credit for my ideas as if they were their own. I lost a tremendous amount of respect for them. To instill confidence in your new leaders, you have to give them credit when they deserve it. And if you don't like their ideas, just thank them for their input and tell them you've considered every angle, and you're going to go with your original plan—this time. No matter what you decide, continue to encourage those growing leaders.

HOW TO LEAD A LEADER: A RECAP

Think ahead. People get sick, and babies aren't always born on their due date. Developing a strong leadership team will help you and others roll with the punches as life happens without leaving your business hanging.

Don't assume. Not everyone wants to be a leader, manager, trainer, or a teacher. That desire comes from the inside, and it usually oozes out of the people who want it, but you have to ask. Invite people into leadership by telling them you think they have what it takes, and then let them decide.

Coach them through fear. Why are kids afraid to take the training wheels off? Why are some of us afraid of the water? Why do some people conquer their fear while others don't? The ones who get over their fear are many times the ones who were well coached. There have been times I found out after the fact that someone didn't step up because they were scared to speak or didn't think they had what it took to accomplish a goal. They were waiting until they hit a certain rank or milestone before taking on a leadership role. What they didn't realize is that the more they do something, the easier it becomes. If a potential leader doesn't make a move because they are afraid, be a coach and help them through it. Say, "You're amazing. You've got this. I'm here with you all the way." Then start showing them what leadership looks like a little bit at a time.

Choose wisely. When selecting new people to develop into leaders, look for the people who show up and step up. Who's volunteering? Who's motivated? And who's collaborating with others on the team? Outside of the job, who is well liked in the community or serves on a committee? These are the people who have natural leadership abilities. Look beyond the résumés and choose the people you want to work with—the people who are doing great things and have the ability to do even more.

Lead by example. Show the people on your team that any of them could be a leader. Instead of telling them what they need to do to be successful, ask them if they want your help. Ask, "Do you want me to show you what I did? Do you want me to help you prepare your talk? I can share what's worked well for me in the past." Even if the person says no, they will appreciate that you asked.

Add perspective. Give your growing leaders a new perspective. They've been viewing the business from their personal point of view, and a second set of eyes can open a new world of possibilities. Say, "Have you ever thought about it this way? Have you ever looked at your numbers like this? I can teach you how to do that if you'd like."

Learn and Teach. If you are the type of leader who keeps all knowledge for herself, you can't wonder why your team isn't succeeding. Your team can't duplicate your systems or learn new skills if you won't share them. When you learn something new, teach your team, and coach them as they learn to master the new skill.

Chapter Fifteen

KEEPING THE LOVE ALIVE

Sometimes, people hit a certain point in their business and think, "This is what I am. This is my business, my team, and my leadership style. Now that I run a thriving business, I'm done putting in work." This is flawed thinking—if you stop doing the work that made your business successful, it will become a thing of the past.

People often highlight the best things they did to get there. That's great, but dwelling on past systems or successes won't build your future. Tomorrow is a new day; leaders and businesses are built and sustained by innovation and continued growth. You need to keep collaborating with others, finding new leaders, and prospecting. All of these actions keep you moving forward.

Think about your relationship, especially if you're married. You used to be in love. You used to have date nights. You used to have sex every week. You used to do all of those things. Now, maybe you haven't done them in months—it's not the same relationship it once was. The love is there, but it hasn't been tended. Just like you need to put the work into a relationship, you need to work on the things that made your business a success in the beginning.

MY RECIPE FOR SUCCESS

There's an old adage that says a person should spend 80 percent of their time prospecting for new business and 20 percent managing and coaching their team. For a leader, that's simply not possible. In the early stages of your business, you're focusing on building new relationships, talking to people, and constantly sharing what you're doing. Remember, though, that there are other important elements needed for success, and you don't want them to fall through the cracks. If one or two are missing, everything can fall apart. This is how I suggest you spend your time growing your business:

- **Prospecting (40 percent)**—Spend 40 percent of your time meeting new people and telling them about your business and products.
- **Marketing (10 percent)**—This is dedicated to social media posting, sending a newsletter, or finding other

creative ways to market your business and keep advertising. Don't let this slip.

- **Showcasing (5 percent)**—Dedicate this time to monthly events, online presentations, or some type of PR event.
- **Self-development (10 percent)**—Self-development is imperative. Read books on how to become a better leader and how to grow a successful business. Work on your mental health, physical health, creating boundaries, and dealing with family and personal challenges when they are present. You can't effectively mentor, manage, and lead others if you're unable to focus on your work. You have to be the best version of yourself to lead others to greatness.
- **Training others (10 percent)**—Training is important, but it can't take all of your time. As you conduct your self-development, naturally share what you learn. There's no need to train others on core habits again and again. Automate a system that trains new people as you bring them in so you don't have to spend all your time on this task. Create videos, manuals, and programs that are easily accessible. Doing so frees you up to continue learning, and you can keep sharing fresh information with your team.
- **Planning (5 percent)**—Plan your day, which sets you up for the week, then for the month, the quarter, and the year. You need to view your business through a macro lens—pull out your calendar and plan according to hol-

idays and yearly trends. Big holiday weekends usually mean fewer workers and fewer purchases, so maybe that's the perfect time for a sale or event. You'll also want to plan your planning time and build your business according to a schedule. For example, if you have your macro schedule in place and you're reading a new book, you'll know that you can read for thirty minutes on two nights per week. If you carve everything out on your calendar, the plates will never stop spinning!

- **Loving on your team (10 percent)**—Loving on your team is so important. Recognition, appreciation, sending love notes, picking up the phone, spending quality time, and posting public shout-outs on social media takes up some time. When you aren't doing it, it should be on your mind. You have to make sure it happens, or people will be unhappy and feel unappreciated. If you're on top and making lots of money, you need to thank the people who helped you get there.
- **Back end (10 percent)**—Managing websites, reports, products, and inventory are all part of running a business, and handling them takes time. If you're no good at it, outsource it to someone else, or else it will take up more of your time than it should. If you hit a wall and say, "I don't want to do that because I'm not good at it," then hire someone! Invite someone over who is good at it and trade skills or ideas. Be resourceful!
- **Rinse and Repeat.**

MAKE IT YOURS

Keep in mind, this is a simple guide. This is the recipe I use to productively allocate my time, but yours could end up looking very different. However, the one element that I believe is absolutely essential is planning. If you plan your days and months according to the needs of you and your team, you place them (and yourself) in a better position for success. I also want to emphasize that you can plan all you want, but if you don't base your business on the people who make it possible, you'll become stagnant. If you plan and lead by example, you'll surely grow a successful business!

SOME FINAL
THOUGHTS

Becoming an entrepreneur changed my life. I've realized I have to continue to develop myself, dig deep to find meaning, and constantly evolve and improve. It has also made me realize that cultivating business relationships is similar to how I'd develop them with my friends or my spouse—through effort and care.

I believe my success can be attributed to my focus on relationships and culture over money and power. When you truly want others to be happy, that's when the magic happens! People come together as a team, and you become an almost unstoppable force. I'm a people person—I love helping others, I love learning more about what makes someone tick, I love knowing that I may have, in some way, helped change someone's life for the better. It's the journey—just like the ups and downs of dating—that creates memories and plants the seeds to whatever or whomever is waiting for you at the end. These relationships fill my cup, and they've helped me build the business of my dreams. There's no greater feeling than when someone on my team succeeds.

I want you to succeed, too.

WHY NOT YOU?

You deserve happiness. You deserve your best life. Why not you? Are you ready to seize your own business opportunity and fall in love with your business and your life? Do this for me today. Say, "What if? What if I put myself out there? What if I prioritize my own happiness? What if I stop making excuses? What if I spread love to everyone around me? What if I say yes to my business and really give it my all? What if I say yes to loving my career? What if I just say yes?"

The advice contained in this book—this guide to growth—helped me to build my business through cultivating relationships and creating an unbeatable culture. I implemented these practices and systems, and they worked for me. I hope you'll follow it to build the business of your dreams with the people you love!

APPENDIX

KEY TAKEAWAYS

Fix what's broken. If you're always in a fight with someone else or upset, you need to look within. If you're in your thirties, forties, or fifties, you should not be having fights with your girlfriends or colleagues. Yes, there can be a tiff every once in a while, but you're not in high school anymore. Grow up.

You are worth it. You only have one life to life. Don't sit around in your sixties and seventies saying, "I wish I had done that. I wish I had made a change. I wish I had tried." Today is the day! Make a change and don't look back. Figure out your number one goal and work to achieve it.

Say yes. When someone invites you, then go. Say yes to

business, friendships, and new relationships. Say yes to the guys or the opportunities that don't wow you on paper. Why? You never know what they might really be like.

Be the best version of yourself. Even when you aren't feeling it, put forth the best version of yourself. Forget about you for a second, and spread a little bit of love every day.

Get healthy. Focus on your health. When you're healthy and confident, you can easily be your best self. Eat well, exercise, and let your confidence spill into every part of your life.

Make connections. Find the people you love and talk to them. Avoid the haters and naysayers, or put them to the side. Reach out to people by sending a card. Call people! Meet one new person each day, and you will grow an amazing network.

Keep your options open. Go out there and play the field. Meet with prospects and team members often. You never know who will be amazing, who will become a great leader, and who will help you build your business. That person who is "too rich" or "too quiet" might be looking for what you have to offer. Talk about what you love about your business and keep opening your mouth until you're comfortable talking about it with everyone.

Analyze everything. Every time you talk, present, or share, look back. What was good? What was bad? What would you change?

Cultivate new business. As you bring in new prospects and team members, be relational. Remember, you're dating them in the beginning, so find out what works and what doesn't. Show them that you are there to support them and use the "we can do this" approach—don't focus on yourself.

Celebrate people. With PDA and appreciation behind closed doors, you can show growing and developing team members that you recognize and appreciate what they are doing. Both shout-outs and private recognition are important, so use a combination of both. Offer incentives—find new and different ways to encourage people to achieve a little more. Find out what they want and use that to facilitate growth.

Show love equally. There's no room for playing favorites. Love on everyone, and give everyone a bit of your time. Of course, you can and will give more to those who deserve it, but don't let everyone know that!

Actions speak louder than words. Even as you're loving on people, hold them accountable for their actions. Show them that your time is valuable. Use tough love to separate those who want it from those who get less of your time. Identify who really wants to grow and then develop those people into leaders.

Planning is essential. Using this book as a guide, allocate your time according to your own recipe. Plan your days, months, and years. Assess how much time you need to spend on each aspect of your business, and then watch it grow!

ACKNOWLEDGMENTS

Team Dreamlife: This book would not exist without you. You are proof that anyone can have success in this business when you believe in yourself and others—and that you can love your work, love the people you work with, and be passionate every single day about what you do. I am nothing without each of you. Thank you from the bottom of my heart.

Randy: From laying eyes on you in college and our ups and downs during our many dating years to becoming your wife and partner in every sense of the word...thank you for believing in me, pushing me, dreaming big with me, and building this crazy beautiful life, family, and business with me. You are my best friend. Our love story fueled so much of the content in this book—it would be blank without you.

Mom and Dad: Thank you for all of your sacrifices, your

support through the years, and your endless love to me, Randy, and my kids. You instilled a fearlessness in me to never give up and to keep going through good and bad, and have been incredible role models on how to live life to the fullest.

Erica: Thank you for being the best sister on the planet. I am so lucky to have you in my life and now around the block. I love doing business, life, and motherhood with you.

Lioncrest Publishing: Thank you for helping me put my thoughts on paper and bringing this book to life. What started as an idea and a dream has become something I can hold in my hands that I am so proud of. To Kayla Sokol, Geneva Ross, and everyone at Scribe Media that collaborated on this project, thank you for your guidance and encouragement through every step of this process.

Kathleen: Thank you for being the best neighbor, mentor, friend, editor, and guide through this process. Your edits and wisdom were crucial, and I would never have started and finished this book without your endless support.

Nan and Scott: Your endless love and support of me and the boys does not go unnoticed. Your passion for social justice and for bettering the world has rubbed off on me, a lot!

My friends and family: Every time you ask me about my

work, it fuels me. Thank you for loving all of me throughout the years. I appreciate each of you more than you know. Every laugh, every tear, every Like, and every time you meet me on the dance floor...you make life so much fun.

Melissa: Thank you for thinking of me when you started your business. I am forever grateful to your countless follow-ups, nudges, and your belief that this could be the answer I was looking for. Cheers to almost ten years of partnership!

Dr. Katie Rodan and Dr. Kathy Fields: Thank you for allowing people like me to partner with you in this business. You have given all of us the gift of entrepreneurship and to dream again.

Sebastian, Darien, and Julian: I love being your mom. I never thought I would have three sons, and I love being the queen of our house. Being your mother has been the greatest job of my life!

ABOUT THE AUTHOR

MIRIAM STEKETEE is a former dancer and corporate gal who turned a network marketing side hustle into a seven-figure business in just four years. She left the corporate rat race in New York City to build a life and career she loves on her own terms, from home. Today, her passion is to help women live authentically and become the best version of themselves, and believes building and maintaining relationships are the keys to sustaining a business long-term.

She lives in Ridgewood, New Jersey, with her three children—Sebastian, Darien, and Julian—and husband, Randy, who was able to start his own law firm because of Miriam's success.

Learn more about Miriam at miriamsteketee.com.

Made in the USA
Monee, IL
05 May 2021